COMPILED BY

SISI SURGANT

SHADES OF SCARS

A Mosaic of Women's Resilience

St. Louis, MO

Published by LBB Publishing. An imprint of Little Black Book: Women in Business

Cover art by Elysia King

Cover, interior, and layout design by Sisi Surgant and Shelly Snow Pordea

Formatting and editing by Shelly Snow Pordea

Photos by Empowering Portrait Studio

Paperback ISBN 978-1-962417-42-6

Ebook ISBN 978-1-962417-40-2

Statement of
Content

This collection contains personal accounts that explore complex and, at times, sensitive experiences, including abuse, trauma, and deeply personal belief systems. Each story is told in the author's own voice and reflects her individual perspective, shaped by her life, her healing, and her understanding of the world.

The views expressed within these pages may differ from one another, particularly in areas of faith, spirituality, and personal interpretation of events. These differences are intentional and honored. This book is not meant to present a single way of thinking, but rather to offer a mosaic of lived experiences, each one valid in its own right.

We invite readers to approach these stories with openness, compassion, and care for themselves as they engage.

CONTENTS

To the women in these pages. From the moment I saw you, I knew there was something special about you. A depth. A story. A strength that deserved to be seen and heard. Thank you for trusting me with your truth. For your courage, your honesty, your voice. You are not just part of this book—you *are* this book.

———

To all the incredible women in my life, especially my mother, my sister, and my daughter. Thank you for shaping me, supporting me, and showing me what it means to be strong, to love deeply, and to rise—again and again.

———

And to women everywhere. Across countries, cultures, and circumstances, to those who are celebrated, and to those still fighting simply to be free, I see you. I see your strength. In all that you carry, all that you endure, and all that you continue to become, there is a power within you that cannot be taken away. And when we stand together, support each other, and believe in one another... something extraordinary happens.

With all my love, this is for you.

INTRODUCTION

BY SISI SURGANT

There is something extraordinary about what has been broken and has found a way to rise again. The kind of breaking that leaves a mark, that shifts something within you, and still allows you to return to yourself in a deeper way.

In mosaic art, every fragment matters. Each piece, with its own color, shape, and history, is placed with care into a larger design. What once felt scattered begins to come together, forming something whole that carries every part of its journey within it.

The women in these pages embody that truth. Each one brings her own story, her own voice, her own lived experience. Some are bold, others quieter, but each carries a strength that stands on its own. Together, their stories form something powerful. A living mosaic that draws you in, where every piece matters and every story belongs.

Across cultures and generations, from the intricate mosaics of Morocco to the quiet, unspoken stories women carry, there is a shared truth. What we live through does not diminish us. It adds depth, strength, and meaning, even in ways we may not immediately recognize.

As you read, you may recognize parts of yourself within these pages. A feeling, a memory, a truth you have carried. And perhaps, in that recognition, something begins to shift.

This is *Shades of Scars*, a mosaic of resilient women, and a reminder that everything you carry has a place, and can come together in ways more powerful than you ever imagined.

Burn Beautiful

by Sisi Surgant

May 18th, 1985. It was a rainy Saturday, the kind of day that makes you want to stay home. The skies were dark, the rain relentless, and the occasional bursts of hail pelted against the car windows as my parents drove. I was just a one-year-old, strapped into the car with my siblings—my ten-year-old brother and my five-year-old sister.

My parents weren't even sure they should go anywhere. My mom actually got very angry about it, and they debated turning around a few times, but they felt a sense of obligation. A family friend was in the hospital, and they wanted to visit him. It didn't feel right to back out, so they kept going despite the bad weather.

What I'm about to share isn't something I remember; it's a story told to me over the years by my mom, dad, and siblings. I was too young to recall any of it, but their memories of that day are vivid. It's a story that shaped not just my life but all of theirs, too.

After arriving at the hospital and spending some time with the friend, my parents decided to stay longer. The friend's wife was alone at home with their kids and felt lonely, and the family friend convinced my parents to keep her company. My dad had to run a quick errand, so he left my mom, my siblings, and me at the friend's house for a while.

I was thirteen months old, sitting next to my mother, on a little chair in my own little bubble of baby thoughts. My sister, five at the time, was playing nearby with our mom's friend's daughter. The two of them were giggling and twirling around, caught up in their own world, until their game got a little too wild. At some point, they picked up a metal bar to play with, and my mom, always quick to react, jumped up to take it away before anyone got hurt.

And in that split moment—while her eyes were on the girls—everything changed.

The family friend stepped out of the kitchen carrying a tray of freshly brewed Moroccan tea. The kind that's super hot and sweetened with thick sugar. She spotted me sitting on the chair and, for reasons I'll never truly understand, thought I was about to fall. That's what she says, at least. So she rushed toward me to grab me, and in the chaos, the tray tipped.

I don't remember any of this—I was too little—but I've imagined it a thousand times. The boiling tea spilled all over me. The scalding sugar clung to my skin. It burned my chin, my chest, my belly, the inside of my legs, and other parts of my tiny body. I don't remember the pain, but the scars tell the story.

The only reason my face was spared is because of my big brother—my ten-year-old hero—who acted fast. They say he knocked the rest of the tray away before it could reach me. I don't remember that either, but I know in my bones that he protected me. He always did. And even though I don't say it enough, I'm so deeply grateful. For that moment. For every moment. For the way he's always shown up for me and still does.

We've always had a bond that words can't fully explain. He's not just my brother—he's one of the first people who ever fought for me.

We don't remember the moments that define us. Not when we're that little. But they shape us anyway.

According to my mom, the room exploded into chaos.

She remembers screaming. Crying. Not the kind of crying where you're still composed, but the kind that pours out from the soul. The kind that comes from watching your baby suffer in a way no mother ever should. The friend who spilled the tea was in complete shock, apologizing over and over again, frozen in place. My siblings—just kids themselves—were terrified. Still. Silent. Eyes wide, unable to process what they were seeing.

And me?

I was crying, my mom said. Wailing in a way she had never heard before. A cry that wasn't just from pain—it was confusion, fear, betrayal by the world around me. My skin blistering, my baby body burning. My tiny world—my soft, safe baby bubble—shattered in seconds. I didn't understand what was happening, but my body did. My nerves were screaming. My soul was stunned. I was in agony, and I didn't even have the words yet to ask for help.

The ambulance came quickly. But the burns were severe—third degree. There was no time to wait. I was rushed to the hospital, and after a quick assessment, they realized I needed care beyond what they could provide. It was life-threatening—they called for a helicopter to transfer me to another facility, every second suddenly mattering.

My parents have told me about that moment many times. About how surreal it was to see their baby—barely over a year old—being taken away like that. My life was hanging in the balance, and there was nothing they could do except pray and trust strangers to save me.

But there's one detail my mom always comes back to.

She says when they laid me down for transport, one of the medical staff—maybe a nurse, maybe a doctor, no one remembers now—sat beside me. And I didn't cry. I didn't make a sound. I just reached for him. My little baby hand grabbed the fabric of his shirt, held on tight, and didn't let go. I stared at him in complete silence, wide-eyed, stunned. Like my body had used up all its noise. Like all I could do was hold on to something—someone—and try to survive.

That image haunts my mom to this day. Her baby girl, burned and broken, clutching a stranger in total silence.

That was the moment she knew things were serious. That this wasn't just an accident—it was a trauma that would live with all of us forever.

I spent the next six weeks in the ICU.

Six weeks of wires, tubes, beeping monitors, and sterile white walls. Six weeks where my little body had to relearn everything it had just barely begun to know. I had to learn how to eat again, how to move again, even how to walk.

I couldn't take anything by mouth at first, so they fed me through tubes. When I was finally able to start tasting again, it was with tiny Q-tips dipped in juice. I would suck on them like a baby bird, one drop at a time—just enough to feel something sweet in the middle of all that pain.

My mom never left my side. Not for one second.

She stayed in that hospital room day and night, holding space for me while juggling everything else. She had to be my rock while still being a mother to my siblings. She was fighting fear with every breath, doing everything she could to make sure I felt safe. And even now, all these years later, when she tells me those stories, she still cries. Her voice trembles, her eyes fill with tears. Because even though I don't remember it... she does. Every second.

She let my brother and sister play in the hospital playground because, in the middle of all this heartbreak, they were still kids. She watched them through the window—her body inside the ICU, her eyes outside on them. Always checking, always hoping they were safe. I can only imagine what that must have felt like—being torn in three different directions, but still showing up fully for all of us. Carrying the weight of my pain, their innocence, and her own guilt for not being able to protect us all at once.

And my dad... he tried to hold everything together. He had to keep working, keep showing up, keep the family afloat—financially, emotionally, spiritually. He bounced between the hospital, home, and work, carrying his trauma in silence, while trying to be there for his wife, his burned baby girl, and his two other children, who didn't fully understand what was happening. He had to be the strong one. But I know it broke him, too.

There was a moment—my mom always brings it up—when one of the doctors looked at her and said, "You know... your daughter's baby fat may have saved her life."

Before the accident, she used to get told all the time that I was too chubby. That I was overweight. That she needed to stop feeding me so much. But ironically, that extra softness—the rolls, the roundness, the cheeks everyone loved to pinch—that might have been what kept the burns from reaching my organs. That softness became armor.

And my mom? She's proud of it. Still. She says, "I fed you so well, baby, I saved your life."

The scars, though, were unavoidable. They stayed. But so did I.

The burns didn't just change me.

They changed all of us.

That day rewrote my entire family's story.

My parents carried—and still carry—a mountain of guilt. Even now, all these years later, they still replay the what-ifs in their minds like a never-ending loop. What if I had been faster? What if I hadn't looked away? What if I could go back? What if we hadn't gone to visit that day?

The weight of those questions broke some of their relationships, too. We no longer speak to the family friend who caused the accident. Not because we didn't try—but because the pain was too deep, the wounds too raw. Some things just couldn't be repaired. There was too much grief, too much blame, and too much sadness sitting between everyone like an invisible wall.

My siblings were just kids, but their childhoods were stolen in an instant.

Suddenly, everything became about me. About poor Sisi. About getting me better. About hospital visits, burn creams, special care routines, follow-up appointments, and making sure I wasn't in pain. They were little—but they had to grow up fast. And even though no one ever said it out loud, I know their hearts carried confusion, jealousy, sadness... maybe even guilt of their own. Everything shifted. And they were left figuring it out in the shadows of my recovery.

For a long time, I didn't feel guilty. I just saw myself as the victim. The little girl who got hurt. The one who was scarred. I didn't know any better.

But as I got older, the guilt crept in. Quiet at first, then louder. Even though I know it wasn't my fault, I started to feel ashamed of all the attention. I wondered if I was worth all the sacrifices my family made. The time, the energy, the emotional toll. My siblings had to grow up faster than they should have. My parents' lives were consumed by my care. And I sometimes asked myself... was I worth it?

And still, when I think of that little baby me, just 13 months old, sitting on a plastic chair one second and wrapped in bandages the next... I can't help but wonder what she went through. What she felt in that moment. What she still carries in her body.

Because I know I carry it.

And something in me changed as I got older. Especially now, being a mother myself.

I started to see my parents differently. When they used to cry while telling the story, I would roll my eyes and think, Oh come on, I'm fine. Why are you overreacting?

But now? As a mom myself.

Now I get it.

Now I feel it in my bones.

Now, when I think of my mom watching her baby suffer, juggling two other kids, she could only watch through a hospital window, trying to smile while dying inside—I want to cry for her. I want to hug that version of her and say, You did so much. You did enough.

I started to see my siblings differently, too. I used to be so caught in my own pain. I couldn't see theirs. But now I do. They were just kids, trying to make sense of why everything changed. Why their baby sister suddenly needed so much. Why their parents were tired and tense, and always busy with me.

And believe it or not... I even started to empathize with the woman who caused it all.

The family friend who made the mistake.

She didn't wake up that morning planning to pour boiling tea on a baby.

But it happened—and it changed her life too.

How do you live with something like that?

It took me years to realize that my scars weren't just mine. Everyone around me carried pieces of them, too.

Empathy became the shift that changed everything for me. It softened the sharp edges of my pain and reminded me that I wasn't the only one carrying it. My parents, my siblings, even the woman who accidentally burned me—they all carried their own version of the trauma. Just because their scars weren't visible didn't mean they weren't wounded.

When you begin to see the story from more than just your perspective, something powerful happens—you stop feeling like you're carrying it all alone. The weight is still there, but somehow, it becomes more bearable when it's shared. That's the quiet magic of empathy. And if there's one thing I believe the world desperately needs more of, it's that—the willingness to feel for each other, with each other, beyond just ourselves.

May 18th, 1985; a rainy Saturday that changed everything. It is the reason I'm a burn survivor, the reason I have these scars. But it's also the reason I've learned to appreciate resilience, love, and the strength of family. It became my superpower. It was a very dark day in my life and my family's life, but it taught me some of the most important lessons I carry with me today.

I no longer look at May 18th as a sad day. I actually celebrate my resilience and my strength that day, kind of like a second birthday.

ABOUT THE AUTHOR

Sisi Surgant is a bestselling author, keynote speaker, entrepreneur, and the founder and creator of MISAJO Sports, a modern athleisure brand rooted in confidence, movement, and self-expression. Known for her powerful stage presence and deeply resonant storytelling, Sisi speaks on identity, resilience, and confidence—guiding audiences to own their story and step fully into who they are.

A burn survivor and third-culture woman raised in Germany by Moroccan and Tunisian parents, Sisi brings a truly global perspective to her work. Fluent in five languages and having traveled to over 40 countries, she bridges cultures, experiences, and identities in a way that connects across audiences worldwide.

Before launching her brand, she worked in Germany within the fashion industry alongside iconic houses such as Yves Saint Laurent Yves Saint Laurent, Calvin Klein, and Filippa

K—bringing both creative vision and industry expertise into everything she builds today.

In her memoir Burn Beautiful, she shares her journey from surviving trauma to stepping into visibility, power, and purpose. In addition to her work as a speaker and author, Sisi is a sought-after stylist and color analyst, helping individuals elevate their presence through intentional style.

Based in St. Louis, she lives with her husband and two children and continues to expand her impact globally through speaking, storytelling, and brand building.

Tiny Doors

by Elysia King

"Thank you for calling Ameren Electric. For billing questions, please press one…" The phone recording rattled off prompts from the tinny cell phone speaker, and I sat frozen, staring into the dark.

I couldn't believe they turned off our electricity.

I had been on three months of medical leave without pay from my nursing job, and my husband's part-time job couldn't even cover our rent. We were already working so hard for so little, and to further complicate matters, we were adjusting to the new dynamic of parenthood.

My six-week-old slept peacefully in my arms while I numbly negotiated a payment extension to get the lights back on. Upon hanging up the phone, I listlessly took in my surroundings: not pitch black, just dark enough to leech all the color from the room. Or maybe that was my own mood. Everything was grey, uncertain, and devoid of life. Postpartum hormones weren't doing me any favors, but I felt completely hopeless.

This wasn't working. Hospital policy wouldn't take away my job entirely, but they didn't have to pay for a new nurse's medical leave. My chosen career path was about taking care of other people, but it wouldn't take care of my family or me when it mattered. I allowed myself to wallow in that knowledge as the exhaustion settled into my bones.

It hadn't always been like this. I felt purpose and pride in my nursing career, and the fast pace of the Cardiovascular ICU kept me motivated. Nursing was a solid choice for my resume, guaranteed work in just about any field, and room to advance depending on the specialty. The daily challenge of twelve-hour patient care was invigorating, and I was proud to tell people I was a nurse.

When I wasn't working, I would paint or draw commissions for clients: risk-free, fun little art projects on the side. I got immense joy from my creative endeavors, but never really took them seriously, even when my nursing friends would tease me that I should become an artist instead. *Really? Whoever heard of a nurse who quit her job to be an artist?*

I had a decent balance of low-stakes art and high-stakes nursing until I got pregnant, then full-time night shifts began to threaten my health. I had to go on bed rest for the last six weeks of my pregnancy, and my paid maternity leave was used up before I could even deliver my baby. Suddenly, I was facing the holes in hospital policies and the utter lack of care for nurses in my position. I guess I assumed the safe career of nursing would set me up for financial success, but the moment my benefits were used up, and the lights went out, I felt like a failure.

I was the type of person who always had a backup plan, a silver lining, a positive spin. For the first time in my life, I couldn't see a way out of this. The lights were literally out, my world was grey, and something had to give.

That was eight years ago, and life since then has felt like a series of tiny doors opening and closing, always shifting, always asking me to step through before I felt ready.

The first door closed quickly when my husband, Derek, and I packed up ourselves and our newborn and moved back to our hometown. We found new jobs, an affordable townhome near family, and settled into our new life as parents. During this healing season, we added a new baby boy to our family, and suddenly, my part-time nursing job was *just* enough income to cover day care expenses for two kids.

The day I was set to return to work from maternity leave after our secondborn, I dropped off the kids, pulled into the office parking lot, and burst into tears. I didn't walk back through those doors. I didn't return to my old nursing job. It was 2019, and although I had no idea what was coming, I knew my life in nursing no longer aligned with the life I wanted for my family.

So I stepped back from the hometown nursing job, and another door closed behind me. Derek was working full-time and thriving in his career, and we decided it was time for me to stay home with the kids for a while. I was also dabbling in some small art projects, and to my surprise, people were actually willing to pay for my work.

When the world shut down in 2020, I was already at home with my kids, but I put in an application to start working in a COVID-19 unit. Due to hospital hiring freezes, I wasn't even able to get a nursing job. It was the craziest thing that doors were closed all around me, despite my having a nursing background to legitimately help in a time of crisis. Everything felt backwards, and I coped by doing random art projects: drawing cats, plants, and scenic landscapes.

At the time, people were stuck in their homes and forced to look at their walls all day, so there was a sudden need for art and decor. With the creative door swung wide open, and a market willing to pay for original art, I jumped in feet first. Even though people showed legitimate interest in my work, art was low stakes, certainly not a viable career path for a woman with a nursing degree. At least, that's what I told myself.

I was making small art projects and raising two tiny tornadoes disguised as children. It was wonderful, exhausting, holy work being at home with my boys full-time. One day, as I was knee deep in laundry and listening to a creative arts podcast, I heard a woman named Chloe talking about her journey as a full-time live wedding painter in South Carolina. She was so successful, and she was looking to start a team of wedding painters across the country.

"Must be nice," I quipped as I wrenched a tiny sock from the dryer vent.

Then I begrudgingly looked up Chloe on Instagram, not because I wanted to judge, but because I liked the idea of connecting with a community of artists. And she talked a big game, so I knew I had to check it out.

When Chloe put the word out online that she was looking to hire prestigious wedding painters, I shoved my foot in that door of opportunity. I messaged her directly and said I wanted in. I had no idea what I was doing, but I had painted at a friend's wedding before and had fallen in love with the process.

In the spring of 2021, I started working as a live wedding painter for Cloud Studio Agency. But, no sooner had I walked through that creative door than I ended up securing a nursing job back in St. Louis. I joined a COVID response team, and since my husband's job furloughed, we switched places: I went back to work full-time while he kept the kids at home with him.

My original plan was to work full-time as a nurse and maybe pick up a few weddings a year. My confidence was astoundingly low, and I honestly didn't think anyone would care about my art enough to make painting a viable source of income.

Thanks to Chloe, by the end of 2021, I was busier painting weddings on the weekends than I was working as a nurse, and I felt so unsettled. I was really proud of the tangible work and purpose in my nursing career, but I was falling deeply in love with the art journey. It took me about six months to realize that I couldn't do everything I wanted to do in my own strength.

I prayed, fasted, and talked to a bunch of people who were smarter than me about what I should do next. Ultimately, I was told not to take any unnecessary risks: nursing was safe. Nursing was necessary. Nurses don't quit their jobs to become artists. On paper, everything I was told was solid wisdom.

I talked to God very candidly about my whole situation, and He answered that I needed to take a leap of faith and trust Him to provide. I told the Lord in no uncertain terms that I would give my all to an art career, and if it crashed and burned, I would go back to nursing. I also gave the Lord six months to prove to me that art was the right choice, as if I were the one setting the terms, and I swear I heard angels roll their eyes. There were no tearful prayers, no solid business plan, just a blind trust to fall through a door I never imagined would open.

Over the next two years, I continued to paint at weddings and events, and my art career started to blossom. I was saying yes to any and everything—from commissioned portraits to interior murals, and my opportunities were not slowing down.

Sadly, my husband, Derek, was not having the same career experience, as his department was dissolved and he was once again left without a job. It was 2023, and despite multiple job applications, there was zero follow-up. Mercifully, my art wasn't slowing down like the rest of the job market, so we crunched the numbers and decided to pivot. We opted to homeschool the kids to coordinate with my work schedule, and Derek took on the role as full-time teacher/stay-at-home dad.

It was not an easy transition from 2024 to 2025. We felt like we were treading water, figuring out how to coordinate work/life schedules while drinking from the fire hose of business building.

Even though things were slowly clicking into place, I was still in a trust fall with no end in sight.

Still, the new art opportunities kept coming. I was getting inquiries from clients, both local and international, for anything and everything art-related.

The art commissions got larger as I partnered with a local nonprofit, LOVEtheLOU, and took on some volunteer mural work. They were able to cover my supplies, and I was able to come up with a concept to transform their blank beige gymnasium walls into a colorful oasis for their students and volunteers to work. That project ended up spanning a couple of years, and it helped me grow immensely in my art knowledge.

God wasted nothing, as each project endeavor led to another opportunity to work with more clients and expand my business. The doors just keep opening to hosting successful art galleries, partnering with luxury clients, painting more walls than I can count, and partnering with artists everywhere. Not to mention doors opening to more than 300 weddings around the world. Even this book cover illustration was another door: an opportunity to showcase the inspiration and strength of a community of women.

I still joke that I'm in a trust fall with God, but I'm leaning into it now. There's an assurance that I'm exactly where I'm supposed to be, and my day-to-day life is filled with color both physically and metaphorically. Thanks to God and the support system around me, my entire family is thriving in this beautiful, crazy, colorful life. But sometimes, I think back to that night.

To sitting in the quiet with my newborn in my arms, listening to the power company tell me our lights had been shut off. To the grey that settled over everything. not just the room, but my spirit. I think about the version of me who couldn't see a way forward, who believed that every "safe" choice had somehow still led her there.

I used to believe progress meant forcing doors open, but I've learned that God opens what I don't have to break down. What I didn't know then was that it wasn't the end of something; it was the closing of a door I was never meant to stay behind. Because the same hands that held that baby in the dark would one day walk through tiny doorways and use her talents to create light.

The same life that felt stripped of color would be rebuilt in bold strokes and wild faith.

And the woman who once sat frozen, afraid of what she had lost, would learn how to walk forward anyway: through uncertainty, through risk, and through doors that didn't make sense until she stepped through them.

The lights came back on eventually. But more importantly, so did I.

ABOUT THE AUTHOR

Elysia King is a registered nurse turned artist based in St. Louis, Missouri, whose work blends intuition, emotion, and a deep appreciation for connection. After years in the medical field caring for others, Elysia found herself drawn to a different kind of healing, one expressed through color. What began as a creative side hustle has grown into a thriving artistic practice, where she creates custom, one-of-a-kind pieces for both residential and commercial spaces.

Her work is known for its ability to evoke a sense of calm, created with the intention of not just decorating a room, but transforming it, inviting conversation and connection. In addition to her commissioned pieces, Elysia has developed a love for creating live art at weddings and special events, capturing moments as they unfold and transforming them into lasting, tangible memories.

As a mother of two boys and a partner in a busy household, Elysia understands the beauty and chaos of everyday life, often drawing inspiration from both. She believes that art has the power to unite people and tell stories without words, and she is committed to bringing that sense of creativity and connection into homes and communities throughout St. Louis and beyond.

I Belong to Me

by Molly Eames

The air was thick and warm, scented with ylang-ylang and plumeria after the jungle rain. Howler monkeys screamed in the distance as mosquitoes buzzed loudly around my forehead, already damp with perspiration. The path down to the *maloka* was rocky and steep. One side dropped into a narrow crevice where we could occasionally hear cattle lowing; the other bordered a low stone wall draped in thick green vines and dotted with vibrant hibiscus.

The descent grew steeper with each step, practically granting permission to pause at the pool on the way back up to the shared accommodations after *ceremony* each evening. I had no idea then how different I would feel after I walked this path again: how my body would be, how much my relationship with myself would change.

Once at the entrance of the sacred ceremonial space, I slipped out of my sandals and set them at the edge of the wooden veranda that wrapped around the enclosure. Butterflies stirred in my stomach: an eager anticipation that felt both grounding and electric. Remembering my mat placement, I stepped through the doorway into the *maloka*, with its carved wooden beams, thatched roof, and open windows, breathing in the night. I made my way to the second mat on the right.

It was simple: a small blanket at the foot and a pillow at the head. Beside it sat a bright red *vomitivo* bucket and a small box containing the essentials of the journey: Kleenex, a lighter, a small red flashlight, *mapacho*, and a pipe. As I settled in, my eyes met the gaze of the person directly across from me, and we exchanged a soft smile that said: *You are not alone. You got this.*

Daylight thinned into a purplish haze, the kind that makes everything feel slightly unreal, and before long, the nocturnal chorus took over completely. It was the only sound left as we quietly and patiently waited for the shamans to arrive.

When it was my turn to receive the medicine and name my intention, I felt deeply grateful for all of the preparation I'd done beforehand. My intention was clear: **I am here to heal.** And I am open to whatever that means for the *oni or the spirit of the medicine.*

Please be gentle, I whispered into the mug filled with a thick, brown, almost-black sludge. I tried not to inhale its potent fumes as I swallowed the viscous medicine. My stomach turned as I forced down a second swallow, making sure that the medicine stayed put.

Immediately, something in me shifted as if I'd been transported to another lifetime. A deep knowing settled into my body: *I've done this before.* The taste was exactly what I expected, deeply earthen and dirt-like. The circle already felt like home.

In the Shipibo tradition, healing is done at night and in silence. The shamans bless the medicine. We speak our intentions. Then, we wait. When they begin to sing their *ícaros,* the songs activate the energetic grid and move through the body like living currents. Precise, ancient, and alive, these songs are potent, magical, and impossibly beautiful.

I lay on my mat, staring at the intricate patterns of the thatched roof for what felt like hours before the maestro and maestra began to sing. The soft crying, the shifting bodies, the nose-blowing around me made me wonder if the medicine was doing anything at all for me.

So I asked my grandmother for help.

She appeared as though she'd just walked into the *maloka,* and gently kissed the top of my head.

"Pumpkin," her spirit said, *"trust this process. I'm here with you if you need anything."*

Her scent, a combination of roses, cigarette smoke, and gin, and the memory of her touch wrapped around me. My body immediately softened. I felt safe. Seen. And ready.

That's when the cold crept in.

It began as a subtle sensation in my toes, slowly climbing up my legs until it swallowed my entire body. My muscles began to shake in tiny pulses, syncing with the rhythm of the *ícaros*. I pulled my blanket up to my chin, wrapped my scarf around my head and face, even covered my nose in a desperate attempt to create warmth. Soon, I was curled into the fetal position, trembling uncontrollably.

That's when I realized: I was frozen. Numb. Empty.

How the fuck did I become a human ice cube?

The more I fought, the colder the room became. My body felt impossibly heavy.

Then a voice, steady and familiar, rose through the static:

Molly, just be in this moment. Stop fighting it. Surrender. Be here.

The voice infuriated me.

As I clenched against the cold, I saw myself as a young girl: playing in the mud, being scolded for dirtying my white shoes and church dress. Tears streamed down my face as the scene quickly shifted. I was five or six years old, being told by my other grandmother that I was not smart or capable. That I was completely unlovable. That I should be grateful to have a sibling who is so talented because I will never know what that feels like.

WTF—why am I seeing this? I muttered to no one.

And that's when it hit me: the medicine wasn't here to break me. It was here to show me what I was desperately holding on to.

This freeze had choreographed my life, keeping me stuck in survival mode.

That's when I dropped into the highlight reel of my worst moments; flung into each memory with no option to fast-forward, skip, or look away. The more I tried to blink the images away, the more I became *one* with them. *What the actual hell*, I thought.

And the maestra's words then filled my system:

A medicine journey is co-created. Ask the medicine questions. Remember your agency.

And the wise voice from within said: *Be here. Surrender.*

Yet, here I am. Frozen in the jungle, witnessing myself in scenes from my past that I wish I could forget. Reliving each scene with subtle differences. My awareness and vantage point broaden so that I could see what else was happening.

Suddenly, I was somewhere else entirely, in a memory that I had tried to bury. Somewhere beneath the *icaros*, beneath the thatched roof and the jungle night, my body remembered.

The clock above my stove was ticking closer to midnight, and I felt sick to my stomach. Tears began to swell in my eyes as I realized my time was running out. The kitchen began to feel claustrophobic, as if the walls were closing in on me. I didn't want to start the new year, *our* new year, our wedding year, with a lie.

Fueled by alcohol and desperation, I blurted out to my fiancé, "I was molested for years..." and collapsed on the floor. As the floodgates opened, held in the arms of the man who had never made me feel unworthy, I told my story.

Then came the fear. And the doubts.

*I am broken. I am broken goods. My life is a complete lie. My family is a joke. Will I ever be **me** again? Will I find peace? Who the fuck am I?*

The welcoming sensation of nothingness began to wrap itself around my shoulders as I leaned into the familiar bliss of being numb.

Oh, how I know this numb space. And cherish it. It's the space that kept me safe. It's the space that helped me survive.

Be here. Surrender to the pain and hurt. Feel the anger, the voice inside of me whispered.

The medicine does not distinguish between then and now. Instead of being an ice cube on my mat in the jungle, it is now 2020, and I feel the cold stone floor pressed against my knees as I wrap my arms around the white porcelain toilet of our bathroom. My body shakes violently while my internal temperature feels like it is a million degrees. Sweat drips down the small of my back. Beads of perspiration gather at my hairline. Tears pool on my upper lip as I quiver with dread. The need to expunge the poison from my body is palpable. I feel the urge rise up in my system as I begin to vomit, again and again, into the toilet bowl.

It's Christmas, and I have to leave our family dinner after barely an hour. I want to be *with them,* but it doesn't feel safe.

My vision shifts, and I'm above myself, looking down at the diorama of the beautiful home that my fiancé (now husband) and I created. On the other side of the bathroom is our daughters' room, and there they are: our children. Our son and two daughters cuddled next to the wall together, listening to my sounds, wondering what was happening, and worried that I might not survive.

How long have I been disconnected from myself?

How long am I going to let this pattern run my life?

Slowly, my awareness is brought back to the *maloka*. One of the helpers is stroking my face and helping me move so that I can receive the sacred songs meant for me. Sacred geometry danced across my vision as I sat up to receive the shaman's *icaros*. With snot running down my face and tears streaming like waterfalls from my eyes, I felt his energetic words moving through me, weaving through my system like cleansing bubbles, scrubbing my insides until they were clean.

With every exhale, I felt the stories of not being enough, of being too much, of being a statistic melt out of my system.

Soon, I was empty. Completely vacuous. No insides, no clenching, no critical voices. No narrative.

Just stillness.

They say that the hardest part of any medicine journey isn't the ceremony itself but what comes after: integration. How will you live differently once you've seen the truth? How will you choose to make the mundane sacred?

A month after returning home, I felt the old current begin to hum.

It started small. An email. A request. A calendar that looked too full. My chest clenched up. My jaw tightened. My thoughts accelerated.

You're behind. You're not doing enough. Move. Fix. Respond. My fingers hovered over the keyboard, ready to fire off three replies at once. My body leaned forward, already bracing.

And then... I noticed. The sensation, not the story. The heat rising along the back of my neck, a faint buzzing in my forearms, my breath shortening into quick, shallow sips.

This is it, I thought. This is the doorway. For most of my life, this is where I would outrun myself. Add more. Do more. Disappear into productivity, or go completely numb while pretending to function.

Instead, I laughed. I let my hands fall into my lap.

The room did not collapse.

I placed both feet flat on the floor and felt the steadiness beneath me. I inhaled, not dramatically, not performatively, but just enough so that I could feel my ribs expand. The exhale trembled on its way out.

My body wanted to surge forward. To prove. To solve. To escape the discomfort of not being enough. But I stayed.

The activation crested like a wave, and without my usual participation, it softened and passed through me. Nothing catastrophic happened. No one accused me. No emergency unfolded. The email waited. The world continued. But something inside of me shifted. I had interrupted the speed. I had chosen slowness.

Not because I was calm, but because I was listening. The medicine had changed me. After reflecting on the whirlwind of experiences it had brought me, I realized I left the jungle with three main understandings.

The first is simple: **Be.** Be here. Now. This moment, this breath moving in and out of my lungs, the subtle rise and fall of my chest, the warmth of the blanket against my legs. This exact configuration of aliveness holds unlimited possibilities.

I feel my toes pressing into the blanket, acting as a tiny anchor, grounding me to the earth. I see with startling clarity that my suffering had never lived in the present moment. It existed in the echo of what had happened or the dread of what might come next. I cannot change what has been done, but I can choose how I meet myself now.

Slowness, once terrifying, no longer feels lazy or unsafe. It feels like relief stretching through my spine. It feels honest. It feels like a homecoming. The tension in my shoulders melts, vertebra by vertebra, as if each had been holding a separate lifetime of worry.

My breath had been shallow for decades, always racing ahead of my thoughts. For most of my life, speed has been my armor. Staying busy kept me from feeling. Moving quickly meant I didn't have to notice the tightness in my chest, the hollowness in my belly, the way my body braced even in moments of joy. Slowing down had always felt like an invitation for everything to catch up to me.

But now, the slowness feels like truth.

In slowness, I can sense my feet touch the ground. I can feel when my shoulders tense and soften before the tension calcifies into pain. I can hear the quiet "yes" and "no" inside of my body that I had ignored for decades. Awareness is no longer a burden; it is permission to exist in the totality of myself.

The second understanding arrived coiled and ancient: the snake.

Growing up in a conservative religious home, the snake symbolized sin, temptation, something to be feared and crushed. After the jungle, it became something else entirely. The snake no longer represented danger; it represented intelligence. Renewal. The wisdom of shedding what can no longer hold you.

I understood, viscerally, that every skin I had outgrown had once saved my life. The numbness. The freeze. The identities I clung to so tightly. They were not mistakes, but adaptations. Staying loyal to what once protected me had begun to cost me my own aliveness.

As I sat to write this last understanding, my arms felt encased, as if something in me still resisted the thawing. My hands tingled, pins and needles spreading from fingertips to elbows. My body was numb, yet somewhere beneath the surface, a river of medicine stirred, moving in waves along my veins like a hidden current. A remembering was happening.

Let go, the voice whispered from deep inside. *Let go and free yourself.*

As the tears streamed down my face, I felt my throat release in small, tremulous grasps. My jaw unclenched in slow increments, my shoulders sagged, and my chest opened. Each shudder, each exhale was a micro release of decades of tension. I felt the weight of old shame pooling in my belly and then dissipating like water sliding out of a cracked vessel. My ribcage expanded, my spine unfurled, my pelvic floor softened. Releasing hurts like crazy and yet also feels like absolute liberation.

Who am I without the trauma title? What shame am I shedding by allowing myself to be fully seen? Whose life might shift because I choose to reclaim my voice and speak the truth?

Each question sent small tremors through my body: a tightening in my solar plexus, a flutter behind my eyes, a subtle pull in my calves. But with every breath, the quivering softened. Decades of holding on reduced to one final finger, white-knuckled and trembling, afraid of what may happen if it finally released.

Letting go was not graceful. It was brutal. It felt like tearing away something fused to my flesh. There is grief in shedding. Grief for who I was. Grief for what that numbness allowed me to survive. And yet, with every release, I feel more access to the vast, quiet intelligence that exists inside of me; the galaxy of wisdom that lives within every human being, waiting for space.

This third lesson had been circling me for years, but I had been ignoring the signs. This realization stripped me bare: I had been more loyal to my trauma than to myself. I knew how to protect it. Defend it. Build an identity around it. But I had not yet learned how to belong to myself. To embrace this lesson was to choose myself fully and without conditions.

Who am I?

I am the woman who no longer abandons herself when things get hard. I am the breath moving slowly in and out of this body. I am the thaw after the freeze.

I am love—not the kind that begs to be chosen, but the steady kind that remains.

I am the daughter who survived. The mother who stayed. The wife who told the truth. I am light, not because I escaped my darkness, but because I walked through it. I am divine, not separate from this body, but because this body survived.

I am a body that learned to feel again. I am not the numbness. I am not the silence. I am not the story that was handed to me.

I am the woman who stays present when every cell wants to disappear. I am grief that softened into wisdom. I am rage that clarified my boundaries. I am a voice that will never go quiet again. But most of all, I am no longer the keeper of my trauma.

It moved through me. It marked me. It changed the shape of my becoming.

But it does not carry my name. It does not own my life.

I belong to myself now.

The moment you reclaim your voice, something shifts. Not just within you, but for everyone who witnesses it. Maybe your own "I am" statements are waiting just beneath the surface.

When they come, trust them. Don't soften them. Don't edit them. They are not suggestions. They are declarations.

They are the sound of you returning to yourself.

ABOUT THE AUTHOR

Molly Eames, M.Ed., is a somatic experiencing practitioner, educator, and intimacy coach devoted to helping people return to their bodies as a source of truth, power, and aliveness. Her work integrates nervous system healing, sexuality, spirituality, and embodied self-expression.

With over a decade in trauma-informed sexual health, Molly guides individuals out of survival patterns and into deeper connection with their bodies, their desires, and their inner knowing. Her approach weaves clinical precision with intuitive depth, creating spaces where play, pleasure, and presence become portals for transformation.

At the heart of Molly's work is a simple but radical invitation to slow down, listen inward, and reclaim the parts of yourself you were taught to leave behind.

Her mantra: Start exploring. Stay curious.

THE HUMMINGBIRD'S GRANDDAUGHTER

BY BECKY WITH THE GOOD LIGHTS

The first time I saw a hummingbird, I was on my Grandma Jeanette's front porch swing in the sweltering, summer heat in the late 1980s. Grandma had a few hummingbird feeders that year, and after a short time, it was as if the entire regional hummingbird population was summoned to feast at our little red-dirt tobacco farm in Western Kentucky. I was mesmerized by the iridescent green glint of their bodies and the contrasting aesthetic against their bright red chests; impressed how one tiny little bird could be so vibrant, fast, and agile. Over the years, the hummingbird population grew with its annual return, each tiny migrant pollinator knowing exactly where to go to satisfy its thirst on its three-thousand-mile journey. Some of the tiny birds acted like they remembered my Grandma specifically, as if they were actually happy to see *her* again, and not just the nectar she provided. At one point, she was even able to hold a few of them in her hands.

My Grandma Jeanette was, unequivocally, my favorite person on the planet. I'd like to think that I was her favorite person, too, but I was the third oldest of thirteen grandkids, and *all of us* were vying for that title. Sadly, metastatic breast cancer took her from us in July of 2012, and while the hummingbird feeders were half-full that day, they certainly felt half-empty. By the time I arrived in Kentucky for her funeral, I had been in the Air Force for almost thirteen years, traveled the world, gone to war, gotten married, bought my first home, had a child, and was a few months pregnant with my second. As I scribbled her eulogy at the airport USO lounge, I was convinced that I could do her justice with my words, explaining how she was the only person to ever teach me that love was a verb and not a noun, and that I was special just the way that I was.

Before closing the casket, my Aunt took Grandma's necklace off and handed it to me; a beaded, 21-karat yellow and white gold necklace I'd purchased for her years prior at the Souq Waqif, or *Standing Market,* during my first deployment to Qatar. Grandma was afraid of damaging the necklace she treasured so much, so she rarely wore it, reserving it only for the *most* special occasions, like her very own funeral. There is a lot of heavy irony in that, so I decided that it would be my duty to live loudly for her and make every day a special occasion. The necklace remains on my neck today, paired with my favorite labradorite stone.

As we laid her body to rest on that hot July day, I stood in my service dress uniform, stone-faced in my shiny black pumps; pregnant and broken, hiding behind my uniform like a shield of professional military bearing. While screaming on the inside and clinging to a fistful of funeral flowers, a hummingbird zipped by... and I knew in my soul that it was carrying her spirit. I just felt it, finding comfort in knowing that Grandma Jeanette was now a spirited hummingbird, spreading her tiny wings for the very first time, leaving that family farm and finding herself in the infinite mystic.

In the years following Grandma's death, life happened fast. I welcomed my second daughter in February 2013. I got orders to Scott Air Force Base in 2015, sold my California house, and moved my little family to Illinois, where I bought my second home. I was promoted to E-7 in 2016 and deployed for almost the entirety of 2017, when my daughters were just four and eight years old. That deployment broke me in ways I didn't know how to articulate at the time.

I divorced in 2018 after ten years of marriage. Military marriages are very difficult, but that is a story for an entirely different book. I paid $1900 a month in alimony for two years, which was thirty percent of my gross pay at the time, and I somehow made it fucking work.

I was promoted to E-8 in 2020 and selected to serve as a Career Advisor for Scott Air Force Base. I applied for retirement in 2021, setting my date in stone for the following year. I found love again in January 2022. I lost my stepfather to a massive heart attack in April 2022. By that fall, I had started a small business building wooden marquee letters with my new love.

It was a whirlwind of a decade, I tell ya!

I finally retired from the Air Force on October 1, 2022, after twenty-three years of service, and found a great job in the IT/cyber field, earning enough to fully fund my business, Get Lit With Life Lights, LLC.

Seemingly, everything was going great until I was notified in late 2023 that my job would no longer offer the hybrid-remote schedule. I'd taken all of my PTO to run Life Lights as a side hustle, knowing that all I *really* wanted to do was be more available for my children at home, bet on myself, and be a full-time entrepreneur rocking vintage with stilettos, after over two decades of wearing camouflage and combat boots for everyone else. My love encouraged me to quit my job, so I did. He proposed two weeks later, on Veterans Day, no less—November 11, 2023—and we were married on March 15, 2024.

Oh, how I wish I had put my foot down and insisted on waiting one more year. Hindsight is a bitch like that, sometimes. But, we turned our wedding into a "Life Lights Love Fest," if you will, and we DIY'd the entire thing to showcase our marquee letters and creative custom builds. It landed us a two-page spread in *Saint Louis Bride* magazine that summer, which was an *incredibly* happy moment for us as both newlyweds and as business owners in the wedding industry. I really thought that we were going to be the next best "power couple" on the Saint Louis wedding scene, and it was absolutely invigorating. But that was not the case...

Before that magazine even hit the stands, our marriage was already on the rocks, unbeknownst to anyone else. Things took an *immediate* turn for the worse upon our return from our Vegas honeymoon, and within ninety days, my new marriage had become my own personal hell. I still do not know the depth of his deception, but the bottom line is that he hadn't filed his taxes in over five years before meeting me, and he still owed thousands of dollars to the state of Missouri from a failed business he and his second ex-wife owned years prior.

This was a huge problem for me, as I'd just handed him a tax return worth more than his *entire* annual gross income for the 2023 tax year, which I'd casually extended filing due to the wedding distraction. It was the perfect shitstorm of nuptial tax fraud, and I was in its epicenter. I very clearly told my new husband, "You have until our first anniversary to get your taxes done. All of them. I can forgive the money that I will never get back, but I *cannot* forgive the deception. You file your taxes, or I file for divorce. Period."

No one can say that I didn't clearly warn him, setting a clear boundary for what I needed from him, in order for us to move forward as a married couple.

Well, he immediately spiraled. He had a drinking problem before I married him, and while he had been disrespectful to me in the past, it was *nothing* like what unfolded in the coming months. He started drinking even more (which I didn't think was possible), heavily abusing his anxiety pills, and threatened suicide multiple times, even texting me, *"you can't pay taxes if you're dead."* As his substance abuse worsened, so did his volatility. What had once only been sharp words turned into unpredictable actions. He spiraled into dependency—on alcohol, on pills, and on control. I don't need to catalog all of the details to tell you it was traumatic. It was. And the hardest part wasn't the chaos, it was the *shame.* I had chosen him. I loved him and knew that he was worthy of love, despite the abuse and deception. I begged him to go to rehab and save himself. He refused. My pride kept me silent longer than I care to admit. I felt that if I left my abusive spouse, I would also be leaving my business and part of my identity behind as well. I simply couldn't face my own darkness.

Though feeling trapped while inside my home, I found a sense of freedom outside, spending almost every daylight hour barefoot in my yard while my abuser was at work, earning money that contributed to *nothing* but his own personal credit card bill. I watered flowers, explored my creek, and tended to broken-winged butterflies as my bank account was hemorrhaging. And, for the first time in a long time, I *prayed* as the hummingbirds darted freely around their freshly filled feeders. I don't really know how to explain it, but in that moment of prayer, I felt my Grandmother's undeniable presence. "Get up, girl," I heard clearly, in her voice. I had nowhere to go, but I physically got up and started healing in the middle of chaos, gaining confidence as I tried to figure out how to spread my wings and save myself.

By the time fall rolled around, things were worse; I had no idea how I was going to get through the winter with no garden to pray and play in. I'd never felt as close to God as I did while in my yard that summer, so I was prematurely mourning that loss, thinking that relationship would somehow dissipate with the warmth of the sun, too. Luckily, it didn't, and during the first weekend of October, a hummingbird returned with a message for me.

A hummingbird in the Midwest in October? That's right. You see, there is another special angel in my life named Jayda. Before I retired from the Air Force, Jayda was a college student and had expressed interest in joining the military. With her stellar military placement scores, I advised her on which Air Force career fields she was qualified for, and which ones were offering hefty enlistment bonuses so that she could make a well-informed decision when I accompanied her and her parents to the recruiter's office. Jayda was incredibly smart and motivated, seemingly born with leadership skills, and I knew that she would be a huge asset to our nation's cyber defense community. She ended up going a different path, finding an incredible job opportunity at Boeing, which I congratulated her *loudly* for when we celebrated her twenty-first birthday.

Just eight short months later, she and her best friend Emily were taken from this earth when they were hit by a drunk driver, only a few miles from Jayda's family home. Both young ladies were barely into their twenties, mere babies on this earth, and neither one survived the crash. Their deaths tore a lot of people's souls in half, and this small town I live in hasn't been the same since that day.

When the regional Mothers Against Drunk Driving (MADD) team came to town to honor Jayda, Emily, and several other local families, I took my illuminated marquee letters there to spell out *MADD* at daybreak. Surrounded by grieving families, the cool October air felt almost too thick to breathe, so I distracted myself at the raffle table. I only had three dollars in cash, which gave me exactly three chances to seal my fate. I placed one ticket in a coffee basket, one in a Harley Davidson basket (*because it reminded me of my stepdad, who passed in 2022*), and one in a Bath & Body Works basket that *just so happened* to have a random hummingbird ornament in it, reminding me of my grandma.

Later that afternoon, I received a phone call stating that my ticket had been drawn! When I met the MADD representative to retrieve my winnings and thank her, I discovered that I'd won the hummingbird basket. My eyes welled up with tears as I took a closer look at the details... hanging from the bottom of the ornament was a little charm that said, "You Are One of a Kind," with a sticker that said, "Trust Your Wings".

When I say that I *heard* my grandmother's voice at that moment, I mean that with every fiber of my being. What I heard sounded more like, *"Girl, you'd better trust your wings and fly out of that mess soon, before it gets worse."* I not only *heard* my Grandmother's voice, I *felt* it, and I understood the assignment. But my schedule was *incredibly* busy at the time, so in true military fashion, I compartmentalized that shit on the spot, and I proceeded to my second marquee setup of the day while my *"business partner"* remained at home, sleeping off his pills and a quarter-gallon of vodka from the night prior.

The very next day, I was invited to a Babes In Business STL event, hosted by the one and only Steph Gold, followed by a private speakeasy-themed sleepover. I was at the event all day, set up my marquee letters, recorded social media content, bought a Babes sweatshirt that said *"Manifesting Epic Shit,"* and had a life-changing *aroma reading* by Shevah of Perfuming Intentions.

Later that afternoon, I realized I didn't have my heels for the speakeasy, so I drove an hour back home to get them. When I arrived, I shockingly found my husband there, already home from work. He was dressed unusually well in a button-down, so I asked where he was going.

He became enraged, yelling, "I am going out, and I think it is *bullshit* that you are putting your *business friends* ahead of your *husband*!" as he stormed out. So, I rolled two joints, found the heels I wanted to wear to the speakeasy, threw them into a backpack with some pajamas, and headed back to the venue. Upon my arrival, I immediately found Steph and explained that I wanted to stay the night, as my marriage was falling apart and I didn't really feel comfortable going home. She agreed without hesitation, so in true veteran fashion, I put on my happy face mask and continued my afternoon as if nothing was wrong.

My business besties and I had a wonderful evening; we even had our own tattoo artist there, y'all! I made fast friends with several women as we sipped curated cocktails, sang karaoke, and shared both laughter and tearful stories of strength and resilience. By the end of the evening, I decided to get a hummingbird tattoo due to hearing "Trust Your Wings" so loudly the day prior. I casually told the tattoo artist (*The Art Doll*), "I'm not gonna tell my husband I am getting this tattoo. I wonder how long it will take him to notice it."

I'd not heard from my husband since his mid-afternoon freak out at the house, but over the buzz of the tattoo machine, my phone began to ding with every drunken text message, each one driving a new nail into the coffin of our dead marriage.

"I hope Steph Gold is worth it."

"Maybe your husband should be worth it."

"Who are you sleeping with?"

"I'm coming to find you. Leaving in five."

"I hope you find your happiness."

And then, in one fell swoop, the coup de grâce...

"We can also discuss how we are going to split the company...I don't trust you anymore."

I immediately responded with "Sounds good. The company is already split forty-nine/fifty-one. You can move out whenever you'd like."

The rest of the night was a blur because I admittedly got incredibly drunk that evening, in what seemed to be the beginning of my own downward spiral. I owe a *debt* of gratitude to the gang of Babes who were there for me that night. I got up the next morning, loaded my marquee letters up, and sent my soon-to-be ex-husband this text at 10:12 a.m.: "Get to packing… I'm headed that way and don't care to see you."

I then posted a reel on Instagram with screenshots of his drunken threats and accusations, drove an hour home, and when I arrived, he was still asleep, having *no idea* that I'd just outed him on social media.

"Get the fuck out of my house, right now," I said, upon entering.

"I'm not leaving. I live here," he protested.

"No, you don't," I said. "You *lived* here, homey… *past tense*. You no longer *live* here, so get your shit and get the *fuck* out of *my* house."

As he stumbled around looking for his morning pills, he yelled something about how he was going to take half of the marquee letters with him. I laughed, making sure he knew that he would get forty-nine percent, *at best*, and that I'd see him in court.

By the time he finally left my home that cold October morning, I wasn't shaking. I was clear. There is a kind of strength that comes from years of military training and compartmentalization, and then there is a *deeper* kind of strength that comes from finally choosing yourself.

In court, he was a no-show, sending an attorney in his place both times. I represented myself, I asked for what was mine, and the judge awarded me full ownership of my business. In the end, the only thing I truly needed from my ex-husband was his absence from my life. The court, thankfully, made that official.

Since our split, I have healed loudly, wildly, and *very* publicly. I've addressed traumas I'd been running from for years, discovering that healing is simply a delicate balance between owning your worth in this world and forgiving yourself for not doing it sooner.

The hummingbird does not question whether it can migrate three thousand miles. It simply moves when the season changes, and I am learning to do the same. What a beautiful sojourn into self-discovery it has been, as I've embraced my new powers as the Hummingbird's Granddaughter who finally learned to trust her wings.

ABOUT THE AUTHOR

Becky Hargrove, also known as "Becky With the Good Lights", is an Air Force retiree, entrepreneur, and creative artisan whose work and writing are rooted in resilience, reinvention, and alignment. She is the founder of Get Lit With Life Lights, LLC, where she specializes in handcrafted wooden marquee letters, custom builds with exciting flair, frequent sarcasm, and brutal honesty.

Following a twenty-three-year military career, Becky transitioned into entrepreneurship as a means of reclaiming her identity, purpose, and joy beyond uniformed service. Her woodshop is a place where her discipline, creativity, and hard-earned perspective intertwine, reflecting her belief that beauty can be built by hand from the remnants of challenge and change. This philosophy carries into her writing, where she explores themes of endurance, healing, and the strength required to begin again.

Originally from rural Murray, Kentucky, Becky now resides in Troy, Illinois, where she is intentionally building a life defined by authenticity, creativity, and connection. She shares her home with her two daughters, two dogs, and two cats, where she continues to create, in both light and in the written language, as a timeless act of resilience and love.

Insecurity Becomes Success

by Natalie Patton

The panic and pressure hit all at once. My thoughts slip out of alignment before I can catch them, and instead of focusing on the moment in front of me, my attention narrows to one uncomfortable place: my stomach. I take a deep breath and tell myself everything is going to be okay. I repeat it again, hoping my body will follow my mind, but it doesn't. My leg bounces under me as I try to steady my nerves, quietly attempting to regain control before it's time to begin.

And then, it is.

My debut television interview on *Show Me St. Louis* begins, and I step into the moment with a smile that feels more practiced than natural. But somewhere between the first question and my first answer, something shifts. I remember how badly I wanted this opportunity, how excited I was to stand exactly where I am, and as I begin talking with the host, Mary Caltrider, about what I know best—creating and selling *all the fun hair things*—and I find my footing.

The words come easily when it's something I love. Bows, headbands, the pieces that bring people joy—it all pulls me forward. My shoulders loosen, my breathing steadies, and the panic that once felt overwhelming begins to fade into the background as confidence takes its place.

By the time the segment ends, I feel a rush of excitement move through me. I'm proud. Energized. Already wondering when I might get to do something like that again. But what no one sees is everything that happens before moments like this, the internal battle that takes place long before I ever step into the spotlight; the quiet negotiations I have with myself just to show up.

I can trace that feeling back to when I was young, sitting in a quiet school library with a test laid out in front of me. White stapled papers, a pencil in my hand, and a room full of students focused on the task at hand. Everything about the environment called for stillness and concentration, but my body had other plans. My stomach twisted suddenly, pulling me completely out of the moment. I remember trying to ignore it at first, convincing myself I could push through, that I could be like everyone else and just finish the test. I shifted in my seat, pressing my legs together, trying to will the feeling away. But the discomfort only grew stronger, impossible to dismiss.

Carefully, I pushed my chair back and walked up to my teacher, trying not to draw attention to myself. I leaned in and whispered, "Can I go to the bathroom?"

When she told me no, something shifted inside me. I panicked.

Was everyone looking at me? Did they hear her say no? What if I can't hold this?

You have to understand that I was a do-gooder. I was the student who followed the rules and didn't cause disruptions, the one who did everything right. And yet, there I was, expected to return to my seat and pretend everything was fine when it wasn't. So I did what I thought I was supposed to do. I went back, sat down, and tried to act normal while my stomach twisted and churned. I don't remember how I finished the test, or if I even did. I only remember the moment it was over, the rush to the bathroom, and the quiet confusion that followed.

That feeling didn't stay in my fifth-grade classroom. It followed me into adulthood, showing up in moments when I needed to feel the most "in control."

It was there even while doing what I love the most: dancing. During my time with Planet Funk, a dance company in Houston, performing in front of crowds ranging from small local groups to massive crowds at a Texans game, *Good Morning America*, *The Debra Duncan Show*, and many others, there it was.

Rehearsals were my favorite part of the week. I loved the rhythm of it, the repetition, the way everything felt predictable and within reach. But performance days were different. There was a shift that happened as soon as the countdown began. The closer we got to stepping onto the stage, the more my body resisted. The ten-second countdown stretched longer than it should have, each moment filled with a growing sense of urgency I couldn't ignore.

I would find myself stepping away, isolating for a moment, trying to regroup before I was expected to walk out and perform like nothing was wrong. And then, just like every other time, the moment would come, and I would do it. I would step onto the stage, hit every mark, move with confidence, and finish strong. When it was over, I would feel the same rush of excitement and pride, wondering how something that felt so impossible minutes before could disappear so quickly once I was in it.

The pattern repeated itself in my professional life. As a manager at a large travel agency in Houston, I was confident in my role. I knew my responsibilities, I respected the executives I worked with, and I took pride in the work I was doing. But before meetings, in moments I was fully prepared for, I would feel the same familiar shift. My body would react before my mind had a chance to reason with it. I would feel the heat rise, the urgency set in, and I would leave whatever I was doing to get to the restroom as quickly as possible. It didn't matter that I was capable. It didn't matter that I was prepared. The reaction came anyway, leaving me frustrated, embarrassed, and searching for an explanation I didn't yet have.

Even moments that were meant to be joyful carried that same undercurrent. Months before my wedding, I found myself sitting in a doctor's office trying to explain a fear that felt irrational even as I said it out loud. I wasn't just thinking about walking down the aisle. I was thinking about what would happen if I couldn't leave when I needed to. What if I found myself standing in front of everyone with no way out?

The anxiety didn't wait for the moment itself to come. It arrived months in advance, settling in and making itself known long before the day ever came. We tried different options, different medications, searching for something that would bring relief, but nothing seemed to fully quiet what I was experiencing.

Over time, I began to recognize a pattern. It wasn't always the event itself that triggered the response—it was the waiting. The anticipation. The space between knowing something was coming and not knowing exactly how it would unfold. That space was where my thoughts would spiral, where my body would take over, and where everything felt the least manageable. It was in waiting rooms, in lines, in moments where stepping away wasn't immediate or guaranteed. That was where the panic lived.

That was the pattern. It didn't matter how prepared I was, how much I loved what I was doing, or how many times I had done it before. My body would react first, and I would be left trying to catch up.

For a long time, I didn't have a name for it. I just knew that in certain moments—especially when I felt stuck, waiting, or without control—something in me would change, and everything would suddenly feel urgent and overwhelming.

Eventually, I learned what it was. Irritable Bowel Syndrome (IBS).

A condition that doesn't follow rules, doesn't wait for convenience, and doesn't care how important the moment is. It shows up when it wants to, often without warning, and once it starts, there isn't much you can do except respond.

Living with IBS means living with that unpredictability. It means walking into a room and immediately scanning for the nearest exit, mentally mapping out how quickly you could get there if you needed to. It means keeping medication within reach at all times, not because you always need it, but because knowing it's there creates a sense of security. It means making decisions that others might not understand—driving separately, choosing seats near the aisle, stepping away unexpectedly—simply to create a sense of control in moments that feel uncertain. It means canceling plans, adjusting expectations, and sometimes choosing not to go at all because the risk feels too overwhelming.

For years, I carried that quietly. I didn't know how to explain something that felt so personal and, at times, so embarrassing. I worried about how it would be perceived, about being seen as unreliable or difficult, about having to justify something that didn't have a clear explanation. So I adapted. I prepared. I managed it the best way I knew how, even when it felt isolating.

Some moments reminded me how little control I actually had. One of the most significant came when the pain changed.

It wasn't the familiar discomfort I had learned to manage. This was different. The pain was sharper, heavier, impossible to ignore. It stopped me in my tracks and made it clear that something more was going on. What I thought was just another episode turned into a series of appointments, tests, and eventually, a procedure that gave me answers I hadn't been expecting.

That's when I learned I had endometriosis.

In the process of removing a cyst, my doctors discovered tissue that had been affecting my body in ways I hadn't fully understood. It was a moment of clarity, but not the kind that brings relief. It was the kind that makes you look back and start connecting dots you didn't even know were related.

Including one I hadn't allowed myself to fully sit with. A year earlier, I had experienced a miscarriage. At the time, I moved through it the best way I knew how, telling myself I would process it later. But learning about the connection between endometriosis and what my body had been going through forced me to look at that loss differently. It wasn't just something that happened. It was something my body had been carrying quietly, in ways I didn't yet understand.

That realization was both heartbreaking and clarifying. Because for so long, I had been trying to separate the experiences—my health, my anxiety, my loss—as if they existed independently of each other. But they didn't. They were connected. They were part of the same story, the same body, and the same reality I was learning to navigate.

And yet, even in the middle of that, life continued.

I was also a mother. I had a healthy daughter, and five years later, we welcomed our son. There can be joy and grief side by side, something I hadn't fully understood until I lived it. The same body that had felt unpredictable and, at times, like it was working against me, had also given me two children. That contrast wasn't lost on me.

Eventually, I reached a point where I knew something in my schedule had to change. Working within a structure I couldn't control meant constantly navigating situations that heightened my anxiety. The "what ifs" became exhausting. What if I'm called into a meeting and can't leave? What if I'm the only one available and I need to step away? What if I don't have the flexibility I need in that moment? The questions weren't constant, but they were present enough to shape how I moved through my days. And in that realization, I began to understand that if I wanted a different experience, I needed to create it for myself.

What started as a small creative outlet quickly became something more. In my living room, I began making hair ties and bracelets, sharing them without fully realizing what I was building. One post turned into requests. Requests turned into products. Products turned into events. And before I knew it, I had created something that allowed me to work in a way that supported both my goals and my needs.

Suddenly, I looked at myself and said, "Natalie, this is it, girlfriend!" I could build my own schedule, structure my days with intention, and create an environment where I felt more in control. The pressure that once seemed overwhelming began to ease—not disappearing entirely, but changing in a way that allowed me to move forward with more confidence.

Recently, I found myself in the emergency room after passing out during an episode, something that had never happened before. Every test was run, every follow-up appointment scheduled, and while the results came back clear, the experience itself was nothing short of jarring. Walking out of that situation with nothing but an "all-clear" meant there wasn't something more serious to worry about, but it also meant this was another thing I would continue to carry.

And yet, something else began to shift. I started talking about it.

What once felt too uncomfortable to say out loud became something I shared, first with a few people, then with more. And in doing so, I realized I wasn't alone. The responses weren't filled with judgment—they were filled with understanding. Stories were shared. Connections were made. And what I had once seen as an embarrassing condition that set me apart became a topic that allowed me to relate to others in a deeper way.

We all have some sort of scar. Hidden or not. Secret or boldly spoken. Wildly noticeable or quietly suffering. Shameful or proud. Wounded or healed. The scars are there. It's who you choose to surround yourself with that helps the healing.

Irritable Bowel Syndrome has shaped me in ways that I did not expect. I now give myself and others grace in situations that I may have ignored otherwise. I rely on my faith, I stay prepared, and I make sure to open up to people, hoping they are understanding of my situation. I have learned to adapt to change, and I have embraced a deep and patient understanding of those who may be silently going through the same (or different) struggles as I am.

Some days my thoughts are quiet, and some days they are piercingly loud, reminding me that: yes, my IBS still very much exists. But, while it exists, it no longer defines me, rather, it serves as a reminder of my uniqueness and how I can be of comfort to others who continue to walk confidently through a scarred, yet fulfilling life.

And this, my friends, is where the new "IBS" comes into play—Insecurity Becomes Success. Let's start our journey on the path to confidence, allowing what we've endured to become part of what drives us to succeed.

Natalie Patton has transformed her experience navigating the challenges of living with IBS into a story of resilience and creativity. As the owner of TOP KNOTch by Natalie, a vibrant brand known for playful hair accessories, she has built more than a business; she has created a sense of connection through what she makes.

While balancing the realities and insecurities that come with IBS, Natalie pours her passion for creation, community, faith, and family into her work. Her products have found a loyal following through local events and a growing online presence, each piece reflecting both her creativity and her determination to keep moving forward. IBS has challenged her in unexpected ways, but she has learned how to shape a life and business that allow her to thrive at her own pace.

Through her creativity, Natalie has connected with people within her community in meaningful ways. In sharing her own vulnerability with loyal customers, she has created space for others to open up about their own hidden struggles. Her story is a reminder that even the scars we cannot see can lead us into something unexpectedly meaningful.

Lose the Plan, Find Your Life

by Erin Fahs

I was twelve years old when I wrote the first list outlining my life.

The plan.

I don't remember anyone telling me to do it. No assignment, no hovering adults, no talk of goals or five-year trajectories. Just a quiet afternoon in my childhood bedroom, surrounded by furniture lovingly restored and passed down through generations, a spiral notebook open in front of me. The house was still, the way small-town houses often are, where silence feels permanent, not temporary.

I wrote carefully, numbering each line as if precision mattered. College. Career. Marriage. Children. Where I would live and when I would live there. The exact order in which it would all happen.

I wasn't dreaming. I was drafting. Trying to escape a foregone conclusion that my life would start and end in the same small town.

Looking back, I'm struck less by the ambition of that list than by the seriousness of it. I wasn't playing pretend. I was trying to solve something, to grasp the future before it could surprise me.

What I couldn't see at twelve was that the plan wasn't built around what I wanted. It was built around *what I believed was expected of me*. What a good daughter does. What a smart student does. What a successful woman is supposed to become.

Dreaming felt indulgent. Wanting something without being able to justify it felt irresponsible. So instead of asking what I wanted, I focused on what would be approved, praised, and look just perfect from the outside.

I grew up in a town of fewer than a thousand people, where relationships are tightly intertwined. People married young, stayed local, and built lives that closely resembled the ones they grew up watching. I can still smell the fried chicken and green beans at those reception hall weddings, and can still feel the rhythm of a community that moved as one body. My friends and I would sometimes crash those receptions as teenagers, sneaking beers, testing limits, and even then, I understood both the comfort and sharp edges it carried.

So, my plan was to get out of there. I felt crowded by proximity. I needed room to breathe.

My parents never applied pressure. They encouraged me quietly and steadily, trusting me to find my own way without attaching outcomes to their hopes. The pressure was entirely my own invention. I looked around and understood, even at twelve, that if I didn't imagine something different, I would simply stay.

I spent my time plotting for the future. For a long time, the strategy—making the plan and working it diligently—worked.

I graduated top of my high school class and headed off to college on a full scholarship. I was in a new world, where the population of my entire high school was the size of my peers' graduating classes. I suddenly found myself surrounded by people who had traveled the world, spoken casually about spring breaks abroad, and had more ease and access than I'd ever witnessed up close. I adjusted my sights accordingly and expanded the plan: adding a second major, taking on leadership roles, and making early mornings and late nights my new normal. I edged toward burnout long before I had language for it.

But empty space felt like a risk. Staying busy was the only way to progress. I told myself that discomfort meant growth. What I was actually doing—I can see it clearly now—was running. Not toward something. Away from something. But running from something you can't name isn't a plan. It's just running.

My senior year brought the first real test. I was accepted into an AmeriCorps program in Washington, D.C. The plan was perfect: one year of public health service, then graduate school, then the rest of my life, neatly assembled, rung by rung. My parents drove me to D.C. with my nominal amount of belongings, and I believed wholeheartedly that everything was finally in motion.

What I found instead was chaos.

The housing was barely livable, cockroaches included. My commute was two hours round-trip on the best of days. The stipend was not enough to cover rent, let alone food and other basic needs. We were encouraged to apply for food stamps and find part-time work on top of our full-time service. None of this had come up in interviews, and I had fully trusted that the stipend would cover what I needed for this year. The people running the program were only a few years older than me; I had mistaken their confidence for wisdom.

D.C. had been on the master list. So I told myself I had to make it work.

After two weeks of watching my bank account empty and my options disappear, I broke. I called my parents and said the words I had never once imagined saying: I can't do this.

They came. They always come. They drove to D.C., packed me up, and brought me home.

That was the first visible crack in the plan.

I spiraled. I cried constantly. I didn't know who I was without the next step on the list. When my mom gently suggested therapy and maybe medication to help me through this season, I cried harder. If I couldn't even start adulthood the way I'd planned, how could I call myself a grown-up?

So, I did what felt safe: I deferred to the next step on the list. I applied to graduate programs and jumped immediately into a relationship, which I now know is a catastrophic idea when you're at your lowest. I was accepted midyear into a Master of Public Health program. I had no money and took on student loans to support myself until an assistantship opened. Promises of that work evaporated when the 2008 economic collapse arrived, and graduating students couldn't find jobs, leaving no positions for anyone coming in. I pivoted—transferred programs, took on three jobs, carried a full course load, and maintained a long-distance relationship. On paper, everything looked fine.

Inside, I knew better. The relationship was wrong. The work wasn't fulfilling. But I was too far in, too invested, too buried in debt and expectation to imagine stepping off the path I'd built. So I stayed. For eight years. Likely, seven too many.

Eventually, I drew a line. He proposed, and shortly after, everything unraveled. In couples therapy, I learned he had been living a double life, including having a child he had never acknowledged or supported. Distance arrived as a relief when he took his dream job in Australia. I tried to build a life in Los Angeles, a city I'd moved to for him. It never felt like mine, even after nearly four years of living there. I knew I missed my family, but I wasn't willing to look closely at my life, feel my feelings, and let go of the plan. I was engaged. So close to marriage and so close to checking one more thing off my life list.

At twenty-nine, I flew to Australia to mark my thirtieth birthday and check on the relationship one final time. Within hours of landing, I knew it was over. I stayed a few weeks anyway, determined to salvage something good from the very long flight and the impending heartbreak.

But when I landed back in Los Angeles, I called my mom. Within twenty-four hours, she was there, helping me sell what I could, pack what mattered, and come home so I could catch my breath.

That was the moment the plan finally, completely fell apart. I had salvaged it multiple times in my twenties, but with a new decade in front of me, I knew on a bone-deep level things had to change, or I would no longer bend. I would break.

Admitting this to myself is the moment my life began.

I want to stop here, because what happened next is the part that still makes me shake my head in wonder. In my thirtieth year, not looking for anything, in fact, actively avoiding anything related to men, relationships, or love—I met my husband.

I had no bandwidth for love. I was focused on healing, on finding myself after years of living according to someone else's expectations. But there are some connections that don't wait for convenient timing. He asked different questions than anyone I'd known—not what we would do, *but how we wanted our life to feel.* What we could build together. After years of having my voice be a secondary consideration, I knew within hours of meeting him that this was my person.

I trusted that instinct completely. For the first time. Four months later, I found out I was pregnant.

This was not in any version of the plan. I hadn't even been sure motherhood was for me. I'd spent so many years focused on achievement and survival that it had always felt abstract, slightly out of frame. But when I saw that positive test, there was no panic. No bargaining with the universe. Just clarity: I am going to be a good mother. He is going to be a good father. We are going to be okay, trusting that what was needed to make this happen would happen.

For the first time, I stopped planning in a linear way and started imagining. It wasn't a checklist, but a feeling. I began listing the kind of home we wanted to create. The values we wanted to model. The rhythm of our days. I could feel something loosening inside me, some long-held grip beginning to release. And what rushed in to fill that space wasn't chaos. It was possibility telling me to wake up and embrace what was actually happening in my life. Not the pre-written, scripted list. I set aside my plan and found a corporate role that would create the foundation for our life as a family.

Life does not unfold according to checklists. It unfolds through connection. Through courage. Through moments that ask you to trust yourself before you feel ready.

My thirties taught me stability. Motherhood taught me surrender. My forties taught me courage.

In the final years of my corporate career, I was doing everything right and going nowhere. Delivering results, exceeding expectations, putting in extra hours, and watching promotions slow, budgets shrink, and people I admired lose their jobs as roles shifted and shrank. Profits climbed for shareholders while the people doing the work were quietly rearranged out of the picture.

For the first time in almost a decade, I asked myself an honest question: Why am I still trading my time, energy, and health for a system that no longer returns the investment?

The answer, when it finally surfaced, surprised me with its simplicity. I wasn't staying because it was working. I was staying because leaving felt unplanned. Here I was meeting myself yet again. When we see patterns repeating, it's important to recognize that it's because we have not fully learned the lesson yet.

I'd spent over thirty years treating the plan as the point. Building my whole sense of safety around structure, timelines, and outcomes I could control. But somewhere in the middle of motherhood, marriage, and watching my forties arrive with a quiet insistence, I had started to change. I had started to trust myself in a way I never had before, not because I had all the answers, but because I finally understood that I didn't need them.

I walked away from a six-figure income and bet on a vision I'd been quietly carrying for years.

Fitness has always been my through line, my creative outlet, the place I feel most myself. Every time I moved to a new city throughout my adult life, finding a studio or gym where I could build community was the first priority once the boxes were unpacked. I knew I wasn't alone in needing that: the warmth of shared effort, the particular friendship that forms between people who show up for themselves in the same room week after week. Making friends as an adult is never accidental. It has to be intentional to grow into something real.

So I bet on that feeling. I combined everything I'd learned across corporate roles, startups, and leadership into something that didn't yet exist. I stopped asking what the plan required and started asking how I wanted my life to feel.

The decision terrified me. It still does, some days. I still like structure. I still appreciate a good plan. But I finally understand that the plan serves the vision, not the other way around.

As I write this, I am opening a second location of my business, La Forme Modern Reformer Pilates. I don't know exactly where this path leads. I only know how I want my life to feel. How I want to show up for people in my life and the impact I hope to create by showing up as the best version of me.

And for the first time, that feels like enough.

That twelve-year-old with her notebook was doing the best she could—trying to protect herself from a future she couldn't see, trying to earn a life she hadn't yet learned to simply claim. I don't regret her seriousness. I understand it. She needed the plan the way a scaffold needs the building—not as the destination, but as a temporary structure to hold things up while something real was being built underneath.

What she couldn't know was that the most important moments of her life would be the unplanned ones. The pregnancy. The man who asked the right questions. The decision to walk away. The second chance she almost missed because she was too busy executing a list.

If you are exhausted, unsure, or quietly longing for something you can't quite name, you are not alone. The people you most admire feel that way too. But one day, when the time is right, I hope you give yourself permission to stop drafting and start dreaming. To name what you want. To trust yourself enough to build it.

The plan will fall away. Your life will be waiting.

ABOUT THE AUTHOR

Erin Fahs is the founder and CEO of La Forme Modern Reformer Pilates, a growing boutique fitness brand with two studio locations redefining strength, community, and personal transformation in the St. Louis area. With more than two decades in the fitness industry and over a decade of leadership experience across corporate, startup, and nonprofit sectors, she brings both operational rigor, values-driven leadership, and heart to her work.

Erin began her career in military health care and exited from global operations for a Fortune 500 company before stepping into entrepreneurship to build something more aligned with her purpose. La Forme reflects that evolution—where structure meets sanctuary and physical strength becomes a pathway to clarity, confidence, and sustainable growth.

Beyond the studio, she is committed to meaningful community impact, supporting organizations that serve women and children.

A mother of two, Erin speaks and writes about ambition, identity, and the courage it takes to release carefully constructed plans in order to build a life that feels fully lived.

SEPARATIONAL STRENGTH

BY SANDY QUMSIEH

Ding ding, ding ding, ding ding... the school bell rings for our usual first-grade lunch. But today? Today is a completely different kind of day at my elementary school in Beit Sahour, Palestine. Today would mark the most unforgettable one of my life, and change everything for my family and me. Instead of greeting my friends and eating my typical salami sandwich outside, I see my seven-month-pregnant mother rushing towards me with a look of fear on her face.

"Sandy!" she calls out to me in front of the crowd.

"Mama, what are you doing here?" I ask.

"Hurry, say goodbye to your friends, we are leaving the country soon!" she says.

"What do you mean, Mom? What is happening, what is going on? Please tell me," I demand.

She grabs my hand as I am trying to hug my friends. Tears stream down my face, my heart full of confusion and so much fear.

I quickly wave goodbye, thinking this has to be a joke. No one has ever mentioned leaving the country to me before. "What about our toys and our life here?" I think.

We rush home, the drive taking only about five minutes. The car is completely silent. When we arrive, we climb the outdoor steps to our two-story home, which overlooks the beautiful fields of the countryside. I open the door and see my grandfather, grandmother, my father, and my younger sister sitting in the family room.

"We're leaving for America," my grandfather says.

The words echo in my head. *America?* A country that feels so far away. The only image I have of America is the Statue of Liberty. I know nothing else.

"But why?" I ask, my voice shaking.

"The soldiers want everything we have, and we must leave to protect our family and our future," he says.

A rush of emotion tears through me. I can't find the words. I am still trying to understand what I have just been told.

We pack our belongings into boxes, taking only what we need to start a new life in America. The plan is for all of us to leave on the same day, but by different routes. My father and grandfather will travel together, and I will go with my mother, grandmother, and younger sister. The plan falls apart the very next day when my mother goes into labor.

As if things cannot get worse, my father and grandfather have to leave as planned, while we stay behind. My father leaves that same night without seeing his newborn daughter.

Our lives begin to take a sharp and painful turn, though we do not fully understand it yet. I say goodbye to my father, hoping I will see him again soon. What I don't know is that in the days that follow, I will say goodbye to my mother as well, without knowing when I will see her again.

Chaos fills our home. With my father gone, my mother tries to keep everything together while we prepare for our next attempt to leave.

When my mother applies for a visa for my younger sister in the following few days, someone secretly informs the consulate that my father has already left the country. Because of this, my sister's visa is denied, and my mother's approval to travel to America is canceled entirely.

We are running out of time and need to leave as soon as possible. Our plan B now consists of separating once again. My grandmother and I will leave together, while my mother leaves for Honduras with my sisters. My mother has a Honduran nationality from her father, and her eldest brother, Raul, resides there.

The night has come, and our home fills with family and friends who come to say goodbye. I cannot stop crying as my cousins try to make me feel better.

My cousin Tamara runs towards me, screaming, "You're going to America! You're so lucky! I wish I could go instead of you!" she says.

"Please go instead of me, we look alike, no one would know the difference," I sadly reply.

I look over the stairway and see a taxi driving up the hill coming towards our house. I now know the time has come when I have to say goodbye to everyone and everything I have ever known.

We gather to step over black coffee, a tradition that symbolizes overcoming obstacles, breaking ties with the past, and marking a clear boundary before starting a new phase. My grandmother and I both step over the coffee and head towards the taxi. I hug my mother so tightly while crying and screaming I don't want to leave.

By force, I find myself inside the taxi. As it drives off, I see my whole life wave at me through the back window. I have no other choice but to accept this reality. I lay my head on my grandmother's lap and cry myself to sleep.

I slept the whole cab ride and woke up at the airport. I help my grandmother carry the bags and head towards the plane. As sad as I am to leave my mother and sisters behind, I have a little excitement to see my dad.

After a twelve-hour flight and a long layover, we finally land in Detroit, Michigan on December 30, 1997.

I leave the immigration line and anxiously begin looking for my dad. I spot him at a distance and run towards him with relief. He greets me with a big jacket, hat, and gloves. I look down at my clothes, and I notice I am wearing shorts and a T-shirt.

"Why are you bringing a jacket for me?" I ask.

"Follow me, " Baba says.

He grabs my hand, and we head out to find the car. Just as the doors open, he says, "Look at this!"

My eyes open in excitement, and I see flakes of white snow falling everywhere! I have never seen snow in my life!

"Wow!" I scream.

I quickly jump into the drifts of fluffy white and start playing. The deep snow reaches my shoulders. I feel as if I were in a snow globe.

Happiness begins to take over me, finally. As we drive home, even as cold as it is, the beauty of the glistening landscape brings some joy to my heart.

We make it home, and I learn that I will be starting school after the winter break is over. I love school so much and am excited to make new friends.

After the holiday break, my dad takes me to school, and I get this butterfly feeling in my stomach. Walking through the halls, it looks so much different than what I was used to back home. There's color, and kids laughing. Artwork of the students on the walls.

We walk into the classroom, and a teacher greets us. She shows me where my desk is. My dad kisses me goodbye and leaves.

"Oh no," I think to myself. I don't speak their language, and I don't look like them. I start to get scared. A group of friendly classmates gathers around me, saying hello and asking me questions in a language I don't understand.

I feel a sense of non-belonging. All of my classmates have blonde hair, light skin, and speak English. I am dark-haired, olive-skinned, and know only three words: home, bathroom, and clock.

I want so badly to get out of here. My stomach feels tight and shaky. I want my mom. I want to go home.

But then a strange thought stops me.

What is home?

I am only six years old, but already the word feels confusing.

I go up to the teacher with my hand on my stomach and say to her, "Home." My father picks me up from school, and I feel every salty tear run down my face as I tell my dad, "I don't want to go back."

Not because I don't like it, but because I don't feel as if I belong. I don't understand anything.

The year keeps moving, despite my protests to turn back the clock. I hate every minute of school. I go home every single day, faking stomach pains, and just trying to be with my dad. I go to school for an hour, maybe two, head to the nurse's office, and then dad picks me up and takes me to work with him. I sit for hours at my dad's job doing absolutely nothing.

As long as I am next to my dad, I feel a sense of home.

Months pass, and my dad spoils me in small ways, buying me my first bike and my first dollhouse. I know he is trying to fill the empty space left by my mom. During this time, she and my sisters are in Honduras with my uncle Raul. My dad buys international calling cards almost every day so we can speak to her and check on the status of her visa. The cards only allow us to speak for a few minutes at a time.

I watch my father closely during those calls. At first, he sounds hopeful. But as the weeks turn into months, I see the frustration growing in his face. Every phone call ends the same way—with more waiting and no answers from the consulate.

Without realizing it, I begin trying to take care of my dad in the small ways a child thinks she can. I try to make him laugh. I try not to cause trouble. In my mind, it feels like it is just the two of us now, and somehow we have to make it work.

Most nights, I fall asleep beside him. On weekends, we ride bikes or go fishing together. Every Sunday, we go to McDonald's, where I discover my love for hamburgers. Slowly, life begins to feel a little more normal.

But the waiting never really leaves. As months stretch into years, something inside me begins to change. I start to distance myself from my mom. The child in me cannot understand why she left me behind.

When she calls, I don't always want to speak to her. Sometimes I hand the phone back to my dad. Other times I stay quiet. I tell myself that if she truly wanted me, she would have found a way to take me with her and my sisters.

At seven years old, I cannot understand the decisions my parents have to make. All I know is that she is not here.

In October of 1998, my mom calls with devastating news. A massive hurricane has struck Honduras and Nicaragua, causing catastrophic flooding and mudslides. Entire communities are destroyed, and thousands of people lose their lives. The government shuts down for months.

Any hope of her visa moving forward disappears overnight. We begin to lose hope. Two and a half years pass this way—one short phone call at a time. Each time the phone rings, my dad hopes it will be good news, but it isn't.

Then one evening, my dad answers the phone, and I immediately notice the smile on his face. For the first time in years, I see excitement instead of worry. This is the moment he has waited for—my mom and sisters are coming to the United States!

I feel a strange mix of emotions when I hear the news. I am happy for my dad. I know how long he has waited for this moment. But inside me, something else is stirring.

How am I supposed to face my mom after she has been gone for two and a half years? Did those years not matter to her? Will she come back and pretend nothing happened, as if we can simply start where we left off?

The angry part of me refuses to accept that.

"No," I tell myself. "Never."

If she thinks she can walk back into my life and everything will be the same, she is wrong. The rebellious part of me decides she should feel what it was like to be left behind.

When my dad goes to pick them up from the airport, I refuse to go with him. I stay home instead. Butterflies fill my stomach as I hear the front door open later that evening.

"Sandy!" my mom calls.

For a moment, every part of me wants to run toward her. I want to hug her and never let go. But I freeze. Instead, I run to my room and lock the door. My mom stands outside and speaks to me through the door, gently telling me that my sisters want to see me.

My heart feels pulled in two directions. After a moment, I slowly unlock the door and step out. For the first time in two and a half years, I see my mother again. My hands wrap around her so tightly. Something inside me softens in that moment, and I begin to believe that maybe everything will be okay.

I walk past my mom and greet my sisters. Almost immediately, I realize something surprising.

They don't speak English. They don't speak Arabic either. They only speak Spanish!

The situation is so unexpected that it actually makes me laugh.

"How am I supposed to talk to my sisters now?" I think.

Soon, our house fills with the sound of Barney playing in Spanish on repeat. Not only am I struggling to learn English at school, but now I am learning Spanish so I can communicate with my sisters.

Before long, I start singing along with the songs and picking up new words.

"This might actually be fun," I think.

In the years that followed, as we faced many challenges in our new life in America, I never allowed anything to defeat me. Every obstacle I encountered throughout my adolescence and adulthood brought me back to that moment in my life. I had once lost everything I had ever known, including myself, but somehow, the pieces of me came together again.

What once felt like an ending became the beginning of my strength. From the ashes of loss, I discovered resilience I never knew I possessed. Each struggle taught me that even when the world is unfamiliar and the future uncertain, the human spirit has the power to endure, adapt, and rise.

Identity can be rebuilt, dreams can be reborn, and hope can survive even the darkest moments.

Today, I stand not defined by what I lost, but empowered by what I overcame, grateful for the new journey, proud of the scars, and confident that no matter what lies ahead, I will always find my way forward.

ABOUT THE AUTHOR

Sandy Qumsieh is an entrepreneur and storyteller whose journey has shaped her strength and perspective. Her narrative, "Separational Strength," reflects her experiences with displacement, cultural adjustment, and family separation.

The challenges of immigration and rebuilding a life in a new country shaped her into a woman defined not by what she lost, but by what she overcame. Today, Sandy writes to honor her journey and to inspire others to rise above adversity with courage, faith, and hope.

For the past six years, Sandy has built a successful permanent makeup business, recognized for her professionalism, precision, and commitment to client confidence. Drawing from her own resilience, she empowers others to feel self-assured and confident, no matter what life brings.

She shares her story to inspire growth, perseverance, and the ability to overcome challenges.

No One Was Coming To Save Me

by Yunuen Orozco

On April 1, 1992, a military-grade weapon was pointed through my apartment kitchen window.

I was fourteen years old.

The Drug Enforcement Administration (DEA) flooded our small South Central Los Angeles apartment with search dogs and shouting men who treated me like a full-grown criminal. They tore through couches, cabinets, and walls, looking for drugs and accomplices. The dogs stopped at the spot where drugs were often hidden, disguised as large, circular cheese shapes I had seen before. There was nothing there that day.

So many terrifying thoughts ran through my mind. *Where was my mom? Are they going to shoot me? Who is going to pick my brothers up from school if I die? Why are these officers so mean—don't they see I'm just a child?*

After the search, a DEA officer told me my mother would be gone for a very long time and that I needed to call an adult. There was no sympathy, no empathy—just sheer anger in his eyes, as if I had personally committed a crime.

"Is this an April Fool's joke?" I asked.

It wasn't.

I remember feeling numb, completely in shock—so much so that I couldn't even cry. *What am I going to do now?* By this point in my life, I was already accustomed to being the adult, filling the gaps left by my parents' addiction and overall absence. By fourteen, my father was completely gone, and now my mother was in prison.

My brothers were eleven and eight. I had managed to get them to school that morning before heading out myself. It was April 1, 1992—and needless to say, I didn't go to school that day.

That was the moment my childhood ended—though, in truth, it had been slipping away long before then.

I was born in East Los Angeles, California, and raised in South Central Los Angeles through my teens—a place where survival was learned early and fear was not optional. My childhood was filled with constant moves, nights sleeping in cars, and long stretches of hunger. Poverty shaped everything.

Both of my parents spent my childhood battling addiction, feeding those needs before basic family needs. I am the eldest of three children, each of us three years apart. I grew up being both mother and father, often the only comfort for my two younger brothers as they endured the same instability alongside me.

I shared messages of hope and perseverance with them, telling them we deserved better, that we didn't belong there. I told them we had to stay focused, get educated, and get out. Most importantly, we could not fall into the same traps.

I didn't understand it then, but I know now: I was chosen to lead, to protect, and to bring light into a home clouded by chaos.

Both of my parents were fighting battles they couldn't win. My father struggled with alcoholism and drugs and later died in his forties from a drug-induced stroke while living on the streets of California, despite my many efforts to help him. My mother's addiction led her to federal prison.

Their absence forced me into adulthood—not because I wanted responsibility, but because someone had to carry it.

What I know now is this: responsibility was not punishment. It was preparation.

After my mother was incarcerated, my brothers and I were taken in by our aunt. Life was chaotic, but we were together—and that mattered. By my early teens, I was already working, cleaning houses to help make ends meet. Those homes became my first exposure to a world I didn't know existed.

I remember staring into refrigerators full of food, touching the softest linens I had ever felt, walking through homes that felt impossibly beautiful. At the time, I thought I was admiring wealth. What I didn't realize was that something deeper was forming—a hunger, a belief, a quiet certainty that this life was possible for me too.

There was one home in particular I still remember. I was hungry that day. When I opened the refrigerator and saw something that looked comforting and delicious, I told myself it would be fine. I was sure no one would notice.

When the homeowner's husband came home, I learned quickly that I had eaten what he had been looking forward to for dinner.

The homeowner completely lost it on my aunt, who was her long-term housekeeper and often brought me along to help. I was yelled at and humiliated by my aunt in front of the homeowner. And for the first time in a long time, I cried.

I felt so ashamed.

I left the house and started walking aimlessly. I couldn't stay there, carrying that embarrassment and guilt. What followed wasn't about the food—it was about shame. The humiliation lodged itself in my chest and shaped a promise I would carry forward:

I would never again allow myself to be hungry—for food, safety, dignity, or choice. And I would never make another human feel the way I was made to feel that day.

Education felt like my only way out. Creativity, music, and theater became my refuge. On top of cleaning houses, I helped run the household and focused intensely on school. I was an AP and honors high school student. In my mind, education was the exit. I didn't yet have language for faith, but I trusted that something unseen was guiding me forward.

My understanding of faith was shaped early and imperfectly. In my parents' search for relief from addiction, we passed through several religions. I attended Catholic, Christian, and Mormon services, hoping—like any child—that something would ease the weight our family carried. From my perspective, nothing ever changed.

Over time, I came to understand that faith didn't live in a specific place or practice. It lived in quieter moments—listening to myself, choosing differently, believing my actions mattered. I began to trust the energy created by intention and movement, by choosing growth over harm. That belief steadied me.

In South Central Los Angeles, awareness wasn't a personality trait—it was survival. You learned which streets to avoid, when to stay quiet, and how to read a room before danger announced itself. My life was threatened more times than I can count. Through it all, my focus never changed: get myself and my brothers out.

When I was around twelve or thirteen, leaving a laundromat one afternoon, a woman clearly high on drugs crossed the street toward me. Her voice rose before her footsteps reached me. What started as words became a street fight.

I defended myself the only way I knew how—skills learned not by choice, but by necessity.

When I looked up, I saw her friends moving toward me. One held a knife. Another shattered a bottle against the sidewalk.

That was the moment I understood how quickly a life could be taken.

The laundromat owner burst through the door, waving his shotgun, and pulled me inside. He didn't ask questions. He didn't hesitate. He saved my life.

Standing there, shaken and silent, one truth became clear: I did not belong in a place where survival depended on seconds and strangers. I needed to get out. So I became useful.

I continued cleaning houses. I watched my brothers. I made sure we stayed on track to graduate. I ran a household the way responsible adults do—except I was still a child.

That's where Wendi found me—though she didn't know she was finding anything at all.

Wendi was a beautiful, successful young professional with trendy clothes, polished nails, and a kind, witty personality. She had a fun way of talking and a gentle demeanor mixed with a *don't-fuck-with-me* confidence. There was a spark about her that made me happy and motivated me to push myself harder.

I always looked forward to cleaning her house. Any chance to talk with her felt like a gift. She inspired me to believe I could one day become a successful woman, too.

Wendi also had the most wonderful, loving pup named Opal. I still remember her vividly and how I promised myself that one day I'd have a stable enough home to have a dog best friend of my own.

During my biweekly visits to Wendi's, I cleaned her home. I played with Opal. Sometimes she talked. Sometimes she listened. She never flinched at my story or rushed to fix it. She simply paid attention.

One afternoon, standing in her kitchen with a sponge still in my hand, she offered me something I couldn't comprehend yet. Her house. In Pacific Grove, California.

She said I could live there, house-sit, and enroll in the local college. Opal would keep me company. She said it casually—like she was asking me to water the plants.

I was seventeen, nearly eighteen. My mother was about to be released from federal prison. Wendi took me in so I would have the chance to start and complete college.

I went from roaches and rats skittering across pantry shelves to ocean air drifting through open windows. From scanning every corner for danger to walking fog-wrapped streets that felt impossibly quiet.

I still vividly remember the first night I stood alone in that Pacific Grove house, terrified and grateful all at once.

No one was coming to save me.

Because I already had been.

That realization became the blueprint for everything that followed.

My brothers graduated from high school. This was one of my earliest life goals. My youngest brother, Estiven, is now a mobile restaurant owner in California and a father to three children: Sophia, Desi, and Lucy. My middle brother, Jesus, has served in the United States military since he turned eighteen and is now also an in-home nurse. He has two children, Lucy and Geronimo.

To say I'm proud of them is an understatement.

I married young. Together, my husband and I built a beautiful life. We raised two incredible daughters, Lily and Bella, now eighteen and nineteen. One is in college. The other is finishing her senior year of high school.

I wanted them to see—without question—that women can do everything.

Sales became my craft. Discipline became my language. Success followed.

We built businesses. We built stability. We built safety.

After retiring from corporate America in 2022, we chose not to slow down. Instead, we invested in short-term rental properties listed on Airbnb and VRBO. Today, we've opened vacation homes in Indianapolis, Indiana; St. George, Utah; Hermann and Columbia, Missouri; Miramar Beach, Florida; and Sedona, Arizona. We've also invested in long-term rental properties in Missouri, Illinois, and California.

Our company is called Scenic Escapes Holdings, LLC. This work allowed me to stay active in business while indulging my creative love of décor and design. I've been able to play with the beautiful styles and décor I remember admiring while cleaning homes in my youth, but have done it with my own style, with a mindfulness for comfort, glamour, and peace. I am beyond grateful for my craft.

On paper, I have arrived.

But success has a quiet way of revealing what it cannot replace.

In 2023, my soul spoke louder than my accomplishments. I felt restless, disconnected, and empty. I had mastered survival and success—but I had never learned how to truly live.

At the same time, my husband and I faced a truth we could no longer ignore. We loved each other deeply, but we had grown into different people. Over a year ago, we chose to part with respect and compassion.

We remain family. We remain business partners. Today, my focus is on building the next chapter of my life—outside the box. My daughters are entering adulthood. I am choosing self-care without guilt. I am reclaiming the adventures I missed by being too responsible too soon.

I was too busy checking boxes. Now, I want to experience everything I missed—without shame and with a full heart.

I was never meant to fit inside a box. I was meant to break them open. My scars are not evidence of brokenness. They are proof of who I was becoming all along.

On April 1, 1992, a military-grade weapon was pointed through my kitchen window, and my childhood ended. No one came to save me that day.

But decades later, I understand what that moment gave me: Clarity. Ownership. Courage.

No one was ever coming to save me—because I was always becoming the one who would.

Lessons I Carry

I've learned that taking care of yourself is not indulgence—it is strategy. Your mind, body, and health are the foundation that carry you through every season of life.

I've learned that kindness is never wasted. You never know what someone else is carrying, and generosity has a way of returning when you least expect it.

I've learned to stop comparing. Comparison creates imaginary rules and invisible boxes that were never meant to hold you.

I've learned that happiness requires honesty. Dig deep. Ask yourself what actually brings you joy—and choose it without apology.

I've learned that change is not failure. You are allowed to pivot, evolve, and begin again as many times as necessary.

I've learned that relationships can end without anyone being wrong. With respect and love, people can grow in different directions.

I've learned to surround myself with what keeps me curious, energized, and alive.

I've learned to rest—not just to recover, but to reset. Stillness creates space for new dreams.

I've learned to keep learning. Books, mentors, teachers, coaches—wisdom is everywhere if you stay open.

And when I feel stuck, I ask myself: *What am I comparing myself to? Who built this box I'm trying to fit into?*

Then I step on it—and move forward anyway.

ABOUT THE AUTHOR

Yunuen Orozco (Yuni) is a real estate investor and entrepreneur originally from Los Angeles, California. She is the owner of Scenic Escapes Holdings LLC, a growing portfolio of long-term and short-term rental properties hosted on Airbnb and VRBO. A proud mother of two teenage daughters, Yunuen is passionate about building generational stability while modeling resilience, independence, and self-belief.

Her writing is for women who were taught to be strong, silent, and self-sacrificing. She believes women are born powerful—and that softness comes after safety, not before.

This chapter is her love letter to her daughters and to every woman who feels trapped inside a life that no longer fits. Her message is simple but dangerous to old systems: **You are allowed to pivot. You are allowed to want more. You are allowed to choose yourself.**

In addition to her business pursuits, she competed in a bikini fitness competition in the 45+ division and is currently training to compete in natural bodybuilding shows in August 2026—continuing to prove that strength, discipline, and reinvention have no age limit.

Pouring From an Empty Cup

by Steph Spiegel

(The names of people and organizations have been changed for privacy.)

I used to believe my experiences were too small to matter. For a long time, I lived as if the depth of my pain needed to be verified by someone with a harder life before it could count. Anytime something hurt or felt overwhelming, I reminded myself that someone always had it worse. I didn't want to be the privileged white woman who complained about discomfort while other people carried burdens I couldn't imagine. I didn't want to be dramatic, needy, or ungrateful, and I definitely didn't want anyone to think I was manufacturing problems for attention. I swallowed everything before the truth even reached my own mind because it felt safer to dismiss my pain than to risk being judged for having it.

Growing up, that mindset became automatic. If someone crossed a line, I softened it through excuses. If I felt overwhelmed, I told myself I was lazy. If someone hurt me, I insisted I was being a little bitch and needed thicker skin. I didn't allow myself to express negative feelings without asking whether I had earned the right to feel them. I became someone who minimized my own reality so thoroughly that I eventually forgot how to recognize harm in real time. It didn't make me strong or humble; it simply made me disappear.

When I convinced myself that my story didn't matter, I stopped seeing myself as someone worth caring for. I ignored my instincts and shrank to avoid conflict; I turned myself into the easiest possible version of myself so I wouldn't cause discomfort or inconvenience to anyone else. The result wasn't resilience; it was quiet erosion.

As a Midwest girl who moved to the Pacific Northwest in her twenties, I felt lonely almost immediately. I was fresh out of college, eager to serve, and even more eager to belong. I had some family in the area, but that didn't fill the ache for peers or friendship. I needed people who understood what it felt like to be in your early twenties, trying to balance work, independence, anxiety, and the pressure to appear whole even when empty. I wanted a place where I didn't feel like I was auditioning for a role I already feared I was failing.

That was the version of me who walked into Safe Harbor Church. I had always loved service-based faith. In my past, I had gone on mission trips, served people experiencing homelessness, and stepped into any space where help was needed. Those experiences made me feel connected to God and to the world, and they made me feel needed in a way I didn't know how to create for myself. Service gave me purpose, and being needed made me worthy of God's love.

Safe Harbor was run by Pastor Paula, who created a modern, welcoming atmosphere that made faith feel accessible and relevant. The community included people of all ages, but had a clear focus on supporting those in their twenties and thirties. That season of life is messy and complicated, and it felt comforting to be around people who understood that reality. I walked through the doors of Safe Harbor, hoping for grounding, connection, and a way to feel relevant the way I always had: through service to others.

Food played a huge role in building the Safe Harbor community. As a congregation, we believed deeply in the power of meals to create connection, and we fully embodied the belief that good things happen when we eat together. As a child of a loving and supportive Italian mother, cooking had always been one of my main ways of showing love, so joining Safe Harbor's meal team made perfect sense to me. The meal team felt like a space where I could contribute in a meaningful way, while doing something I loved.

The meal team was run by Diane, who had a strong personality and a direct communication style. She knew her limits, and she said no when necessary without guilt or hesitation. I admired that quality because it was something I had never learned to do. I felt obligated to say yes to everything, and the idea of disappointing anyone terrified me. Diane didn't operate with that fear, and while I respected her for it, I didn't yet understand how essential that skill would become in my own life.

Diane and Pastor Paula often clashed because the expectations placed on volunteers were intense. Paula wanted a level of structure, consistency, and output that was hard for anyone to maintain while also trying to balance life, work, and relationships. Diane eventually reached her limit and decided it was time she stepped away.

We met for happy hour to talk about what might happen next. I walked into the conversation thinking she needed someone to cover temporarily, but as she spoke, it became clear she was handing me the role entirely. She framed it as something I should feel honored to accept, and I nodded because saying no felt impossible. I didn't volunteer. I was assigned the responsibility, but I internalized it as something I should have anticipated and gladly embraced.

Stepping into the role of Meal Team Leader was overwhelming almost immediately. I'm no stranger to logistical issues, as my professional background was in operations. I felt confident that I could fix any of the team's ongoing frustrations by implementing a system that worked for everyone. The biggest issue seemed to be surrounding communication. Trying to find a system of sharing responsibilities across the rest of the meal team was scattered, and expectations were messy. No matter what I did, someone was inconvenienced. The frustration from the team was constant, and although I tried to organize systems and create clarity, every attempt ran into resistance. Email was inconvenient, apps were confusing, text threads were too chaotic, and spreadsheets were ignored. The issue was not the tools, but the unwillingness of people to adjust their habits, and the result was a steady stream of unconstructive criticism that always found its way to cut me down with passive-aggressive comments, intentionally leaving me out of important conversations, questioning my intelligence, and implying that I was lazy and uncommitted.

Pastor Paula added to that atmosphere in ways I struggled to articulate at the time. She spoke in calm, measured tones that made her guidance sound supportive, yet I left every conversation feeling smaller. She would listen as I talked about work, relationships, and life in general, but somehow always seemed to only take away one thing from our conversations: Because I had other large commitments outside of Safe Harbor, I was too young and distracted to fulfill her needs. She talked about commitment and trust in ways that implied I was falling short. She spoke as if I owed more of myself to the church and as if my inability to stretch beyond my limits was a spiritual problem. Never mind that I had just poured my heart out about feeling overwhelmed in life; If I didn't shift my focus to solving the impossible puzzle of the meal team, I was letting her down.

The implied guilt seeped into my faith. I began to believe that if I had stronger faith or more devotion, I would not be so depleted. I wondered if exhaustion was proof that I was failing spiritually. When Paula expressed disappointment, it felt like divine judgment. I accepted her tone as a reflection of how God must see me, and that belief drained me even further.

The stress became physical before I realized what was happening. My stomach tightened whenever I saw a message from anyone on the team. My chest carried a constant heaviness. I woke up tired; no matter how long I slept, my appetite faded, and my mind was foggy. One night, I stood in my kitchen holding a head of lettuce over a cutting board and realized I had been staring at it for an unknown length of time. Rest felt irresponsible, and stillness felt dangerous. I believed that if I slowed down, forgot something, or made one small mistake, I would disappoint people who had already made it clear that they were watching for those mistakes.

During this time, my boyfriend (now husband) was in an intense military training program that required him to be off-grid for long stretches of time. Long-distance made me cling even tighter to anything that filled the silence. I stayed busy to avoid feeling the ache of missing him, but that busyness turned into overworking, and the overworking turned into burnout. I poured myself into my job, the meal team, and anything else that demanded my attention until I no longer had anything left to give.

My breaking point came during one of Pastor Paula's spiritual check-in walks. In the early days, those walks had grounded me. On nice days, we would circle the neighborhoods near the church and talk about life, faith, and leadership. Somewhere along the way, our schedules grew crowded, and those conversations disappeared, so when she asked if we could reconnect, I welcomed it. I was hopeful to feel heard again by someone whose guidance I had once trusted deeply. But that afternoon, the conversation turned in a direction I never expected.

As she was so good at doing, Paula listened as I talked about the heaviness of life: what was going right and what was going wrong. I caught her up on my relationship and the life I was building outside of Safe Harbor. That's when she said something that shifted my perspective into a birds-eye view to see what I should have seen from the start. She said that while new relationships can be fun and exciting, I need to be careful that I don't get distracted from what's really important: my service to the church. The more she spoke, the clearer her message became. The life I was building beyond the church wasn't something to be respected; it was something to be corrected.

What shook me most was not the criticism itself, but the authority behind it. Pastor Paula wasn't just a supervisor or colleague in my life. She was someone who spoke about spiritual calling and obedience with the confidence of someone representing God's voice. So when she questioned my priorities, it didn't feel like a disagreement between two people. It felt like a judgment on my faith.

By the end of the walk, the ground beneath me felt different. The same words that once felt like guidance now felt like a verdict: that my relationship, my work, and the life I was building outside the church were somehow less faithful.

The pain of that realization landed deep and stayed with me, and forced a shift in my thinking. I finally asked myself why I was giving everything to a place that not only devalued my effort but also minimized all aspects of my life that didn't directly involve the church. Why had I tied my worth to my degree of usefulness to people who didn't respect me? It was about damn time I acknowledged that the fear of disappointing people had controlled far too much of my life. I realized I had built my identity around being agreeable, adaptable, and easy, and I had drained myself dry in the process. I had been pouring into others for so long that I didn't notice my own cup had nothing left.

Stepping away from Safe Harbor took time, and it was frightening because I had built so much of my life around that community.

I began paying attention to the heaviness I felt after certain interactions. I became more aware of the knot in my stomach that tightened when someone asked something of me that I didn't have the energy to give. I learned to say no, even though it made me uncomfortable. I had to teach myself that self-preservation was not selfish and that setting boundaries was not the same as failing.

It wasn't a clean break, and it definitely wasn't brave at first. Stepping back looked more like a quiet tapering that I disguised as being busy. I answered messages later. I stopped canceling my own plans to fill in when no one wanted to show up for the team. I excused myself from conversations that once felt imperative. I had invested so much of myself into those relationships that walking away felt like abandonment, not self-preservation. I didn't want to seem dramatic or ungrateful. I didn't want to lose people who had once felt like home. Like so many people do in toxic relationships, I created distance in small, cautious steps, hoping no one would notice the shift. And as I slowly pulled back, I realized something even more unsettling: I had spent so many years bending myself into what others needed that I couldn't tell where their expectations ended and I began.

My shift away from Safe Harbor Church made me recognize something even deeper. I had confused the voices of flawed people with the voice of God. I had allowed human disappointment to become spiritual guilt. I had taken responsibility for dynamics that had never belonged to me. I had accepted exhaustion, burnout, and emotional depletion as spiritual tests rather than as signs that something needed to change. I had put all of my effort into filling other people's cups without recognizing that my own had been empty for as long as I could remember.

It took a long time to understand that my boundaries are not selfish walls to break down, but signs of self-respect. They're a way of acknowledging my own humanity. They're my only way of protecting my energy so I can offer something meaningful without losing myself.

I began to start noticing how my chronic people-pleasing addiction was just that: a disease that left me feeling depleted, worthless, and depressed when I perceived even the smallest bit of disappointment directed my way. Safe Harbor wasn't the origin of those patterns in my behavior. The church didn't create the part of me that struggled to rest or the instinct that told me I had to earn my worth. Those parts were a product of years and years of learned behavior. The people of Safe Harbor just took advantage of my fear of failing others so far that it became a catalyst for the change my life needed. Unhealthy expectations pressed against habits I had carried my entire life, and the pressure made it impossible to pretend those habits were harmless. I was suddenly forced to see the ways I had abandoned myself long before anyone else could. That realization became the first step toward reshaping my life in a way that went far beyond walking away from a church community.

Even now, I still catch myself wanting to say yes before I consider the cost, but there's more awareness now. I force myself to pause and check in. I have to consciously assess whether I have the capacity to give what is being asked. I remind myself that I can't offer anything meaningful if I run myself into the ground. I can't pour into others if my own cup has nothing left to give. I am still growing, still adjusting, still trying to find balance. My spirituality is something I'm rebuilding slowly and carefully, separating the truth of my faith from the voices that once misrepresented it.

I still believe my purpose in life leans heavily toward helping others and showing up for people when they need support, but I no longer believe that kindness requires me to abandon myself. When my cup is full, the care I can offer others is steadier, softer, and far more genuine than anything I could give when I was running on empty.

So, my message to the people I love, and have yet to love, is this:

Your story matters even when it feels ordinary. Your boundaries matter even when someone else sees them as inconvenient. Your needs matter even if they do not align with other people's expectations. You can't pour into others when your cup is dry. You can't sustain connection when you abandon your own well-being. You can't build a meaningful life by erasing yourself in the process. Replenishing yourself is not indulgent; it's essential. It's the only way to remain whole. It's the only way your compassion stays alive. It's the only way you remain capable of offering love without losing yourself. Fill your cup because helping others grows from nourishment, not depletion. Fill your cup because you're worthy of being full.

Fill your cup because you were never meant to live empty.

ABOUT THE AUTHOR

Steph Spiegel is a designer, writer, and entrepreneur whose work is shaped by a lifelong curiosity about how people learn, adapt, and make sense of themselves. She grew up moving around the United States, with Minnesota as the one place she stayed long enough to call home. She earned a Bachelor of Arts in Psychology and Business Administration from the University of Arizona, followed by a secondary degree in User Experience Design that deepened her commitment to research, empathy, and thoughtful, human-centered systems.

Steph writes from the perspective of someone who has spent years untangling old habits of people-pleasing, overextending, and perfectionism, while her professional design work centers on helping her clients reconnect with the joy, clarity, and sense of purpose that first inspired them to create something of their own. That intention guided her in building Intervyx Design Co, where she supports business owners through intentional branding, web design, and custom merch that reflects who they are and how they want to show up.

Outside her studio, Steph loves reading across many genres, connecting with her community of womxn entrepreneurs, and exploring new hobbies with her husband and their growing family of rescue animals.

What Broke Me Also Built Me

by Laurie Robinson

Some childhoods gently guide you, teach you safety through repetition, and give you a soft place to land. And then there are childhoods like mine, the kind shaped by instability, unpredictability, and the quiet tension of never knowing what version of the world you would wake up to. Mine was spent waiting for people to be who I needed them to be, even when they never could. Where the air carried questions instead of answers, and love felt like something I had to earn rather than something given freely.

People like to say that childhood ends when you age out of it, but that's a lie we tell ourselves to feel better. Childhoods don't disappear; they attach themselves to your ribs. They follow you into adulthood, into relationships, into motherhood, into every decision, especially the ones you think you're making independently. They become the blueprint for your fears, your expectations, your instincts. They shape who you trust, how you love, what you tolerate, and the version of yourself you believe you're allowed to be.

My childhood was filled with quiet questions no child should ever have to carry—questions I was already trying to answer on my own by the age of nine. I wondered whether I'd have clean clothes to wear, something to eat for breakfast, or if I'd make it to the bus. I worried about whether I'd have lunch to take to school, and whether my friends noticed that I almost never did.

There was never a steady routine, never those small, precious moments children need—like hearing "I love you" after curling up together for a bedtime story. I was learning how to manage pieces of life that most children are never meant to handle alone. So I learned to hide the little things I believed were "normal," blending in on the outside while feeling anything but on the inside.

By fourteen, I was smoking, sneaking into bars, and running with the wrong crowd—choices that slowly pulled me away from school. When it came down to working full-time or continuing my education, I chose survival. While my friends sat in classrooms planning their futures, I was caught in a cycle of drinking, smoking, using drugs, and searching for love in all the wrong places, mistaking attention for affection.

The result is predictable in hindsight: one can either distrust everyone or trust far too easily.

A Lesson in Trust

I wasn't naive, but I was afraid to disappoint, afraid to be abandoned, and afraid that conflict would turn into something I couldn't escape from. I became the quiet, withdrawn girl who apologized for taking up space. The one who didn't know how to stand up for herself because she had never seen what healthy boundaries looked like.

My first real relationship began when I was seventeen. At the time, I truly believed it was love because it looked like what I had grown up knowing. I didn't have a healthy example to compare it to, so the intensity felt normal, even comforting. When I was with him, I felt chosen, wanted, and I was desperate to hold onto that feeling. Little did I know that what I was being given wasn't love at all. It was control masked as love, being pushed around, told I wasn't good enough, called names, and held to impossible expectations. Still, I bent myself in every direction trying to meet them, believing if I just tried harder, loved better, or became smaller, it would finally be enough.

By the time adolescence bled into early adulthood, I continued to gravitate toward relationships that mirrored the chaos I grew up knowing—loveless, distant, unstable—each one quietly reinforcing the belief that I was undeserving. One after another, they showed me the kind of disappointment I had learned to accept, even come to expect, as pathetic as it was. How could I recognize healthy love when unhealthy was the only language I'd ever learned fluently?

So, I stayed small. Small enough to be overlooked, small enough not to make a ripple, small enough that even my own needs barely whispered. I remember my 19th birthday—how I had waited to see him, the most recent in a line of nobodies, hoping for proof that I mattered. Imagine my disappointment: no card, no gift, not even a "Happy Birthday" tossed my way. My chest felt tight, my words thrashing, my heart pounding like it refused to be ignored. But I swallowed it. I smiled. I nodded. I told myself it wasn't worth the storm that would follow if I let the truth out. So I shrank. Smaller. Quieter. Invisible enough to be tolerated. Safe enough to survive.

Then I met someone else—"Him," the one I believed I was destined to be with, and in what felt like an instant, everything changed. I moved into his home within a month of meeting him, and was pregnant with my first child just five months later. Everything I had grown up knowing made these decisions feel normal, mature, even inspiring.

Motherhood Before Myself

I was not emotionally or financially prepared for motherhood. Honestly, I wasn't prepared for adulthood at all. I was still trying to figure out who I was, sculpting my identity out of shards of survival. But when a new life enters the picture, survival stops being just about you.

When I found out I was pregnant at twenty-one, something primal in me activated. The world didn't suddenly become clearer, but my purpose did. I knew how to guard myself, and quickly created a mental list of what I never wanted my children to feel. I knew what I had to refuse, what I had to change, and what I needed to become for them, even if I didn't yet know how to do it for myself.

People hear the word *toxic* and think of something explosive and loud: obvious rage, fights, broken glass, and slammed doors. But that's not the kind of toxic that nearly destroyed me.

My toxicity came dressed as subtle erosion.

The kind that wears you down grain by grain until you don't even notice the pieces of you disappearing. The kind that convinces you that your silence is noble, that your endurance is love, that your shrinking is loyalty. And the hardest part is that I accepted it. Because any kind of love felt better than nothing at all. So, I told myself: "I will adjust. I will make myself easier, quieter, and more agreeable. I will convince myself that this is normal love."

I became the woman who held it all together on the outside, smiling, functioning, showing up. While privately unraveling in ways no one else could see. Anxiety became my shadow. Even the smallest things, an unexpected noise, an unanswered text, or a change in plans could send my heart into my throat.

I wasn't living. I was enduring.

The Quiet Collapse

There is a moment many women experience, though very few talk about it. It's not a breakdown; it's quieter than that, more intimate. It's the moment you look in the mirror and genuinely don't recognize the eyes staring back at you. You tilt your head, squint, lean closer, but the reflection feels like a stranger wearing your face.

That moment came for me when I finally stopped and looked. *How the F did I get here?* The question didn't come with judgment. It came with realization.

The collapse of my identity didn't happen overnight. It was a slow accumulation of moments, tiny shifts of awareness, brief flashes of clarity, whispers that grew louder each time I ignored them. Moments that said: *you deserve better,* even when I didn't believe it yet.

Those moments multiplied quietly until finally, they became impossible to ignore, an accumulation of truths I could no longer outrun: My kids deserved a mother who lived by example, not a mother teaching them how to survive the way she did. Not a mother teaching them silence. Not a mother teaching them to replicate her wounds.

The Turning Point

I remember the exact moment I woke up and reclaimed my life. I had just come home from a week-long business trip. He was sitting on the couch watching TV. There was no "How was your trip?" No "I missed you." No acknowledgment at all.

I walked into a house of complete chaos. Dirty dishes in the sink, the laundry untouched, garbage overflowing because it was all waiting for me. The unspoken message hung heavy in the air: it's *your* job. The kids ran and wrapped their arms around me while he continued to stare at the screen, as if I hadn't even walked through the door.

In that moment, something inside me shifted, like a lock turning after years of being stuck. As my children clung to me, their arms tight around my waist, I felt it in my bones. I deserved more than this. And more than that, they deserved to see their mother believe she did.

Belief arrived slowly, like light slipping through a crack in a closed curtain. As I began to stand a little taller inside myself, memories rearranged themselves. The way I never questioned the late nights because it was easier when he was gone than when he was home. The way I did not dare examine the subtle shifts in his behavior too closely. The way I trained myself not to ask, not to push, not to know.

Each small truth led to a larger, more terrible realization. I could feel it forming, heavy and undeniable, but still I stayed quiet. I swallowed my words. I carried it alone. Seventeen years of taking it all in silence had made the way we were living feel almost natural.

Then one morning, he walked into the bedroom and said, simply, "I'm done."

I looked up at him, and to my own surprise, I smiled. Not out of spite. Not out of anger. Out of relief.

"Me too," I said.

It felt as though something massive cracked open inside the room. The weight of seventeen years lifted from my shoulders in a single, thunderous release. I could breathe in a way I had forgotten was possible.

And then it came. All of it. The anger I had buried. The frustration I had swallowed. The disgust I had refused to name. It rushed through me like a flood breaking past a dam, fierce and unstoppable.

For the first time, I did not push it down.

Building My Life From the Ground Up

When people talk about "choosing yourself," they say it like it's a simple flip of a switch. But choosing yourself is a series of decisions made over and over again, even when it's uncomfortable, even when it's terrifying, even when you don't feel worthy of that choice.

Most of my decisions were made while crying in the shower or staring at the ceiling at 2 a.m., wondering if I was strong enough, capable enough, worthy enough. But each one built a layer of strength I didn't recognize until much later.

I had no roadmap for where I was going. What I had was determination and the growing understanding that the life I wanted would not be handed to me. It would have to be built brick by brick, boundary by boundary, choice by choice.

And I didn't step into this new life gracefully.

I stumbled, failed, and learned the hard way more times than I care to admit.

I learned how to manage finances without falling apart.
How to balance motherhood, a home, and work.
How to discover who I was outside of survival mode and outside of relationships that defined me by what they took rather than what they gave.

Each small victory, a paid bill, a peaceful morning, a moment of clarity, was a step toward rebuilding myself into the woman I was meant to be. A woman who was wiser, stronger, and far more intentional.

I learned to trust my judgment.
I learned that "no" is a complete sentence.
I learned that my voice didn't just matter; it deserved to be heard.

I also learned that love truly exists. That it's compassionate, patient, and deeply caring. It's something worth opening your heart to, and worth surrendering to without fear. And when it's real, you realize it was always meant to be... even if it took forty-two years to find it.

Finding Purpose

Sometimes the most meaningful paths are born from the moments when life forces you to start over. What first felt like loss slowly began to reveal something else—a vision. Not just a job or a career, but a purpose rooted in the very experiences that once shaped and challenged me.

Growing up in instability shaped the way I learned to move through the world. I didn't grow up with emotional support or guidance, so from a young age, I had to rely on my own thinking. I had to figure things out as I went, trusting my instincts even when I wasn't completely sure what the right decision was. There wasn't anyone consistently there to help me process things or show me the way forward, so I learned to observe, think through situations on my own, and make the best choices I could with what I understood at the time.

When I became a parent, those experiences influenced everything about how I raised my kids. I was extremely protective of them because I knew what it felt like to grow up without the support and stability every child deserves. I didn't want them to have to navigate life the way I did. I felt responsible for being involved at every level of their lives—guiding them, supporting them, and making sure they had someone present who was paying attention to what they were going through.

I didn't rely on someone else to raise them or to step in and fill those roles. Their father provided a steady income, but the parenting, the guidance, the emotional presence, and the day-to-day responsibility of raising them fell to me. I was the one paying attention to what they needed, making decisions, setting expectations, and making sure they were learning how to grow into capable, responsible people.

Because of that, I stayed deeply involved in their lives. I wanted them to grow up with a sense of support and direction that I didn't always have. I wanted them to know that someone was there paying attention—someone who cared about the choices they were making and the people they were becoming.

Looking back, the same instinct that helped me survive my own childhood also shaped the way I parented. It pushed me to be present, protective, and intentional about the environment my kids were growing up in. I knew what instability felt like, and I was determined that my children would grow up with a stronger foundation—one that helped them become the successful people they are today.

That same awareness eventually shaped my career as well. I understood what it felt like to live disconnected from my body—overwhelmed by life and numb to my own needs. After my separation, I began to realize I was meant for something more. I started searching for a path that would allow me to create something meaningful.

What I found was a calling to create a space where people could finally exhale. A place that didn't judge their past, their exhaustion, their stress, or their insecurities. Through my own journey, I discovered how powerful it is to feel cared for, grounded, and present in your own skin.

That realization inspired me to build an environment of healing that goes beyond the surface—reaching inward to the parts of ourselves we often hide from the world. What began as a personal search for growth and connection slowly became a passion for helping others slow down, feel safe, and reconnect with themselves.

Today, that vision lives in the work I do. My goal is simple: to create a space where people leave not only refreshed on the outside, but lighter, calmer, and more at peace within.

Healing in Layers

Healing comes in layers, some soft, some sharp, some easy to release, and others deeply buried, waiting for the moment you feel strong enough to face them.

Motherhood healed parts of me I didn't realize were wounded. Independence healed parts of me that had been broken for years. Love healed parts of my fragile heart. My career healed parts of me through purpose, connection, and service.

Healing isn't forgetting. It's understanding your past without letting it control your future.

Rewriting My Story

When I look back at the girl I used to be, the one who walked on eggshells, who stayed quiet, who blurred her boundaries, who believed exhaustion was the price of love, I don't feel shame anymore. I feel compassion.

I want to tell her that she wasn't weak; she was building resilience she would one day need.
I want to tell her that she didn't just survive, she would rise. I want

to tell her about the career she'd create, the home she'd build, the confidence she'd grow into.

Nothing about where I am now happened by accident. It came from choices, from courage, and from refusing to stay where life tried to keep me.

I didn't get here because the Universe handed me peace. I got here because I refused to give up on myself, even when I didn't know what the next step looked like.

Still Rising

My story isn't finished. Like so many of us, I am still evolving. I'm discovering who I am beyond the circumstances that first shaped me.

These days, the life I live reflects who I am rather than the chaos I came from. If you've ever tried to rebuild a life after instability, you know how deliberate that process becomes. Over time, clarity can replace confusion. Confidence can appear where fear once lived.

Looking back now, I don't think the heart of my journey was the struggle itself. Struggle exists in many stories. What mattered was the decision to transform in the middle of it—to refuse to let the hardest parts of my past define the rest of my life.

Maybe *what broke me also built me*, not into who I was, but into the woman I was always meant to become.

ABOUT THE AUTHOR

Laurie A. Robinson is an entrepreneur, wellness professional, and educator devoted to helping individuals reconnect with their bodies through intentional, results-driven care. With a background in sales and customer service, her early career as a Business Development Manager built a strong foundation in communication, trust, and relationship-driven work. This experience ultimately guided her into the health and wellness sector. Today, her work blends strategic insight with a deeply calming, restorative approach focused on whole-body support.

Grounded in the belief that true wellness begins with safety and presence, Laurie's philosophy centers on mindful care, consistency, and long-term vitality rather than quick fixes. Her work emphasizes clarity, integrity, and education, empowering individuals to better understand their bodies and cultivate sustainable self-care practices.

Writing has become an extension of Laurie's mission and a meaningful way to share her story. Through honest reflection and lived experience, she seeks to give voice to the lessons learned along her journey, both personally and professionally, while encouraging others to slow down, listen inward, and lead with intention. Through her work and writing, Laurie continues to advocate for a grounded, intuitive approach to wellness that honors the connection between physical health, emotional balance, and personal growth.

Hiding Behind My Reflection

by Andrea Denningmann

(The names of some people have been changed for privacy.)

A loud crash hit the outer side of my bedroom wall, the one that backed up to the living room. I froze in my bed, tucked under the covers, with birthday gifts still gathered near the foot of my bed. Only hours earlier, the house had been filled with laughter, candles, and the soft glow of celebration. Now the night had splintered apart. Angry shouts cut through the thin wall, followed by the sharp sound of something striking and falling to the floor. Fear crawled over me.

My bedroom door was just enough ajar to let in a sliver of light. Across from me, my sister's door was cracked the same way. We always left them like that, tiny openings between us, escape routes that made the dark feel less lonely.

On the floor beside my bed sat our favorite toy, a lime green Sesame Street rotary phone, bright and cheerful, Big Bird on one end and Ernie on the other. The two phones were connected by a long cord that stretched from my room to hers, our secret lifeline that let us whisper and giggle long after we were supposed to be asleep. It made us feel connected even when the world around us didn't.

Another shout rattled the wall. I pushed back the covers and crawled toward my doorway. Through the crack I saw her. My sister knelt frozen in her own doorway, blankie clutched tight against her chest, scared and confused, trying to understand voices that were supposed to make her feel safe.

"It's okay," I whispered, even though I didn't fully believe it. "I'm here."

We spoke softly across the hall from each other, just enough to feel less alone. Then I told her my plan. We both knew how to move through the house without letting the floors creak. So when the voices in the living room rose again, I gave her a slow, reassuring nod.

She slipped from her doorway and stepped across the hall, her blanket trailing behind like a shadow, as I opened my door wide enough for her to slide through. When she reached my room, we tiptoed to my bed, her small body trembling. I wrapped my arms around her, pulling the blanket over both of us.

Outside our door, the shouting went on, echoing through the walls of our childhood. But inside my room, we created a tiny island of safety, two little girls hiding from a storm they were too young to understand. In the dim light, holding my sister close, I tried to cling to the sweetness of the night we had before, the one filled with birthday candles and wishes, until the house grew quiet and we drifted off to sleep.

When my dad wasn't at work, yelling was the background music of my childhood, especially after my parents thought we were sleeping. Doors slammed, words cut deep, and silence taught me to stay quiet long before I knew what that meant.

My parents loved us, but their love was bruised and battered by anger and brokenness. I was only an infant when my mother suffered a major stroke, one that changed the course of both our lives. She relearned how to speak and rebuild her daily rhythms, and it took grit and determination. Qualities she would later pass along to me.

After overcoming multiple strokes, my mom began to suffer from depression and anxiety, a kind of darkness that never lifted. I feel that, because of these issues, my dad, though not a bad man, made choices that tore our family apart.

Life moves forward in that quiet way families do, even when everything feels uncertain. As I grew, before I was old enough to understand much of anything, I had already slipped into the role of caretaker. I helped my little sister, comforted my mom, and did whatever I could to steady a home that never stopped trembling. Things happened to me that I don't like to remember. The timelines are confusing to me, tangled in the tension of my parents' constant fighting and their eventual separation.

After my parents separated, we began spending a lot of time with extended family. In my mind, how much time elapsed has been blurred, so I cannot pinpoint exactly when these next traumas occurred, but I know it must have begun around the age of eight or nine.

I am choosing not to share who this person is because he was close to our family and a child himself. My intention is not to shame him publicly, but to speak honestly about an experience that shaped my childhood and my healing. I can't even recall the first experience. I was so confused by what was happening that I blocked most of it out. I think the abuse occurred during the time when my parents were separated, possibly during the season when my dad was out of the picture for a few years. Years that were already filled with fear and instability. I was a year older than him, yet I kept wondering why I couldn't stop it. Why couldn't I speak up? Why couldn't I make it end? None of it made sense to me then, and for years it left me feeling disgusted, ashamed, and alone. The mental fog that followed those years, along with the shame and guilt, became almost impossible to carry.

As I got older, I tried to make sense of something no child should have to decode. I spent years trying to understand what happened. Was it something he had seen or experienced? Was it curiosity he didn't understand? I still don't know. What I do know is that as a child, I was confused, scared, and left to carry the weight of something I could not make sense of.

Those questions lingered long after the moments. They settled inside me, shaping how I saw myself and how I moved through the world. I learned to hide behind humor and a practiced smile. I learned how to become the reflection everyone expected, rather than the child who was breaking inside. It was the only way I knew how to survive. My reflection became my shield, my disguise.

When the truth was finally revealed, relief and shame arrived together. I felt grateful the hiding was over, but ashamed I had carried it at all. I thought the worst was behind me. I thought that chapter had closed.

But life doesn't move neatly. Pain echoes.

My parents divorced the year I turned ten. It is one of the few clear timeline markers I can recall from my childhood because it happened the same year as the Great Midwest Flood of 1993. I already felt years older than my age. I watched my mom break beneath the weight of her heartbreak, and I stepped into the role of helper, planner, the little girl who grew up too soon. I learned to stay small to keep the peace, hold my breath when things got tense, and disappear into whatever version of myself made things easier for everyone else. And while I was strong and a fighter in many ways, I was also incredibly shy. I learned to hide behind my own reflection.

But even in the middle of all that pain, God was quietly planting something inside me, a seed of faith, a whisper of hope. I didn't know it yet, but He was preparing me for the woman I would become. I found Him when I didn't know who else to turn to, when my thoughts felt too heavy for anyone else to hear. I was in eighth grade when I gave my life to Jesus. I didn't fully understand what it meant yet, but I trusted him. When no one else felt safe, He did.

Once I reached high school, I slowly began finding myself. It felt like a sliver of light breaking through years of darkness. I formed meaningful relationships, the kind that made me feel seen. Little by little, I broke out of my shell, and for the first time, I felt like myself. I truly believed the past was behind me, but pain has a way of resurfacing when you least expect it.

I remember the day clearly. A warm, ordinary afternoon, sunlight spilling across the pavement as I walked to my best friend Ami's house. She had invited her boyfriend James, and he brought Kyle, the neighbor boy. It struck me as strange because we rarely hung out with Kyle. He was a few years older, part of a different circle, someone who drifted in and out of our world but never fully belonged to it.

Still, I noticed him. I was drawn to his piercing blue eyes and the sharp angle of his jaw. I had a small crush I never admitted to anyone, drawn to the mystery that surrounded him. For a moment, it felt like four teens joking, laughing, pretending to be older than we were. Then the energy in the room shifted. Ami and James slipped away into her bedroom to do exactly what teenagers think they are ready for, leaving Kyle and me alone.

Kyle and I began joking around, and together came up with a plan to make Ami and James uncomfortable, or at least annoyed enough to stop and come back out with us. We walked down the narrow hallway, my fingertips brushing the cream-colored walls as we walked toward her bedroom but instead of going to her door we walked quietly into the first bedroom which shared a wall with Ami's and started bumping the wall, making sexual noises and mocking them, trying to make light of the awkward situation and hoping it would break up the moment. It was all supposed to be a joke. At least that's what my plan was.

But something shifted almost immediately. The laughter faded, and the room took on a different weight. Kyle's expression hardened, and there was something nearly feral in his expression. At that moment, he was no longer joking. He suddenly turned serious and redirected that energy towards me. His voice barely above a whisper, but it carried a strange authority as he said, "We should do it for real," and before I could process what was happening, he began inching me toward the bed. There was no real conversation, no pause for me to think. It was as if he had already decided what came next.

He now towered over me, causing me to fall back onto the bed, and beginning to unbutton my jeans, sliding down my zipper, and forcefully pulling them down. Instant terror shot through me. I was naive, caught off guard, and completely unprepared for any of it. Everything shifted so quickly, and I knew that I wasn't in control. I gripped my jeans before he could get them all the way down and, with as much strength as I could muster, began pulling them back up, hands shaking and forcing out a joking, nervous "No, I don't think so." I wasn't going to let this happen to me, not again. Voice quivering, I said, "I've got to go." I slipped away, and once I reached the front door, I ran hard and fast, the one block to my house stretching like a mile. My mind raced the entire way. He didn't follow. Thank you, Jesus. But the shame followed me. The questions followed me. *Did I lead him on? Was this my fault?* I tried to reason it away, to rationalize the entire situation the way young girls are conditioned to do.

But the truth came later, clear and sharp. I saw it in his piercing blue eyes, the intensity and the intention behind them. When I said no, he didn't stop. When I pulled away, he pushed forward. I will never forget the way he looked at me in that moment. I will never forget those eyes.

I was lucky to escape, but that doesn't erase what almost happened or the way it etched itself into my memory. What makes it even harder to hold is knowing that my best friend was not as fortunate. After her boyfriend James left, Kyle stayed behind. He waited. And he raped her instead.

When she told me what happened, another wave of shame and guilt crashed over me. All I could think was "It was almost me. It was supposed to be me." My mind spiraled with questions I had no way of answering. Why hadn't any of us seen the danger standing right in front of us? I tried to make sense of it, searching for a logic that simply didn't exist. Ami carried wounds far deeper than mine. Trauma had threaded itself through her life long before that day, but that part of her story is hers to tell. What I came to understand is that pain does not dissolve when the moment passes. It reverberates. I learned that in a way I will never forget. And the echoes didn't stop there. They followed me into moments I never expected, including one night still carved into my memory.

One night, after being out at an event, I approached my front door, and immediately sensed something was wrong. At first glance, it looked like two perfect handprints pressed against the glass, a deep red shape that didn't register as anything more than a smear of color. But as I stepped closer, the truth sharpened.

It was blood. Two handprints, dragged downward across the glass, streaked in crimson.

My heart dropped. I opened the door and found my mom waiting inside, tears filling her eyes. "Honey," she said softly, "Ami is in the hospital. She tried to kill herself."

In that moment, I felt the world tilt. Ami wasn't allowed to talk to anyone outside her immediate family, but she was my family, too. I needed to know if she was ok, if she was safe, if anyone could tell me what had actually happened. I was devastated; I wasn't there for her in her moment of need. She came to me for help, and I wasn't home.

She was released from the hospital a few days later, shaken but alive, and eventually she shared her story and her pain with me in her own words. I learned that she had run straight to my house for help, leaving those bloody imprints behind as the only clue of her desperation. It was the kind of detail that sears itself into your memory because even though I hadn't witnessed it, I could feel the fear she must have carried in every step. Those imprints became the silent reminder of a girl I loved unraveling in real time and of a world that suddenly felt far more fragile than I had ever understood before. Those handprints stayed on our front door for what felt like weeks before they were finally wiped away, yet even then, the image never left me. It remained etched in my mind as a constant reminder of her suffering. And somewhere inside me, I held on to the belief that if she could survive what she carried, then maybe I could survive mine too. Still, I didn't understand why pain always seemed to find its way into our home, how innocence could be taken so easily, so quietly. Silence became the language in which we spoke about it, a shared understanding that needed no words. And shame settled in deeper, like a shadow I couldn't shake.

And then I discovered the thing that finally pulled me out of the shadows. A spark that ignited something inside me, a passion that felt like it had been waiting for me all along. In high school, I finally found my grit and determination in my job. I began working at Express, a trendy clothing store in the mall. I had something to prove to myself and to others, and this job helped me to build myself back up. It lit something in me I didn't know I was missing, a calling that felt both new and deeply familiar. But it wasn't until I landed my job at Express that I truly understood its power. Fashion became my escape and my passion. Almost overnight, everything changed. I felt confident in a way I never had before, capable in ways I had only hoped for. Clothes became more than fabric; they became freedom.

Every outfit I styled became a form of self-expression, a way to rewrite my story. Fashion became my armor. If I looked put together, maybe no one would notice how broken I felt inside. If I looked confident, maybe I could convince myself I was. Dressing up became my quiet rebellion, my way of saying: You can't take this part of me.

But as I grew older, I began to realize that the reflection I worked so hard to perfect was never the real me. Beneath the layers of trend and confidence was still that little girl, the one who wanted to be loved without fear and to be seen without performing.

It took years of unlearning to understand that my worth wasn't something I had to wear. It wasn't in the clothes, the compliments, or the approval I chased. It was in the hands of the One who had been there all along.

When I finally looked in the mirror and saw beyond the reflection, I realized the beauty I had been searching for wasn't on the surface at all. It was in my survival. It was in my strength. It was in the way God turned every broken piece into something whole. For years, I hid behind my reflection. I now know it was never something meant to be hidden.

I built my boutique business, Addi & Ains LLC, and my personal styling services to help women heal from trauma, step into their authentic selves, and build confidence through style and self-expression. Every woman deserves to look and feel her best, and I began this work with that belief at the core of everything I do.

While I cannot change the past, I can help women move forward with intention. Fashion does not have to be something we hide behind. It is a great tool to use to help build confidence, create self-expression, and provide empowerment. I once used fashion to conceal my reflection. Now, I use it to shine, and I help other women do the same.

Every woman walks through her own trials and tribulations. Each carries a story that deserves to be honored and told. My hope is that by sharing mine, I can encourage and empower women with similar experiences to rise from their ashes, reclaim their narrative, and become the women they were created to be. My prayer is that women like me use their trauma as fuel to build the life, the family, and the future they dream of.

ABOUT THE AUTHOR

Andrea Michelle Denningmann is a wife, mother of three, and faith-rooted entrepreneur who believes true beauty begins within. Her life is anchored in family, from dance rehearsals and basketball games to quiet prayers whispered in the in-between moments. These everyday rhythms have shaped her heart for women who are learning to balance calling, confidence, and identity.

As the founder of Addi & Ains Boutique and a personal stylist, Andrea blends more than a decade of experience in retail, buying, and brand management with a deeper mission: helping women rediscover who they were created to be. She believes style is not about chasing trends but about alignment. When a woman's wardrobe reflects her identity and season of life, confidence follows.

Through personal styling, closet edits, branding sessions, and special event styling, Andrea walks alongside women in transition, whether they are building businesses, raising families, changing careers, or healing from past chapters. Her approach is thoughtful and faith-driven. She listens well, asks meaningful questions, and helps women shed both outdated clothing and limiting beliefs.

Andrea's story is one of becoming. Becoming courageous. Becoming secure. Becoming bold enough to help other women rise. Her heart is simple: that every woman should feel beautiful, confident, and fully herself, exactly as she was designed to be.

Beauty Born in Darkness

by Sherrie Anderson

I used to brush my mother's hair in the dark. No lights. No words. Just my small hands moving slowly through strands that carried the weight of everything she had endured. It's one of the most sacred memories of my life. I would stand behind her, careful not to pull, careful not to hurt her, careful in a way only a child who has learned to be an adult too early can be. I was trying to make her feel loved. To make her feel safe and seen. I didn't have the language for any of that then. I only sensed that in moments of quiet, care mattered, and tenderness could exist even in broken places. Love doesn't need permission or perfection.

I didn't know it then, but those silent moments with my mother were the beginning of my calling.

My childhood was shaped by instability: homes changing, food not always guaranteed, in a single-parent household, doing everything it could just to keep standing. Spanish was the primary language spoken in our home, and survival often felt like a daily negotiation. Responsibility wasn't something I was taught; it was something placed directly into my hands. By the time I was twelve, I worked to help pay for my siblings' clothes, food, and shelter. I learned early that if I didn't step up, no one else would. Childhood wasn't something I was afforded. It was something I sacrificed so my family could endure.

My mother carried more pain than anyone should ever have to hold alone. Abuse followed her, first from my father, and later from a second husband whose violence nearly took her life more than once. I watched fear become routine. I watched survival become normal. And eventually, I watched pain look for a place to go.

In my mother, that pain found refuge in alcohol.

Addiction was not her weakness. It was her attempt to drown what she was never given the tools to heal. I watched her struggle quietly, bravely, heartbreakingly, and still loving us fiercely even as she was losing herself. I saw strength and suffering coexist in the same body. I learned that loving someone doesn't always mean you can save them.

Fight or flight became my baseline long before I understood what trauma was. My body learned before my mind ever did. I learned how to read a room instantly, anticipate danger, and how to become small or strong depending on what survival required that day. I learned that silence could be protection. And yet, in the darkness, there was beauty.

For me, beauty became not surface-level, not vanity, but as the kind of radiance that restores dignity when life has tried to strip it away. It gave me a way to create calm and safety where chaos once lived. In the salon I have created, I learned how to hold space for myself, and eventually for others.

Because of my mother's tumultuous relationships, abuse shaped the early years of my life. I couldn't always see it, but the tension was always felt, a fear that lived in my chest, and the way my body learned to brace before my mind could react. I remember hiding with my siblings, holding them close, teaching silence as if it were a language that could save us. I became a protector before I understood what I was protecting us from.

The beatings. The screams. The terror of not knowing how far it would go. Those things leave marks that don't fade with time.

I learned how to read danger in tone before volume. How to measure footsteps. How to sense when it was time to disappear. Fear rewired my nervous system, but it also sharpened my perception. Responsibility came early. Courage came without permission.

When my mother finally found the strength to leave, it wasn't an ending. It was a beginning layered with uncertainty. Survival still required constant adjustment. Safety felt fragile. But freedom, even imperfect, was still freedom. We were no longer trapped, but we were still healing.

My mother was incredibly strong. She fought every day to keep us going: fed, clothed, and moving forward. But strength has limits. Years of abuse live in the body long after bruises fade, and when pain has nowhere safe to land, it looks for relief wherever it can find it. Alcohol became her way of coping. Not because she was weak, but because she never believed she was worthy of healing.

Then came the moment that changed everything. There was unexplainable knowing... A feeling settled in my chest so heavy it stopped me mid-breath. Something was wrong. Instinct drove me—the kind that comes from growing up trained to sense danger before it speaks. I didn't question it. I followed it. I went to find her.

What I walked into is something my body remembers even when my mind tries to forget. My mother was lying on the floor, her body still, her face swollen, blood everywhere. For a moment, my mind could not make sense of what I was seeing, as if reality had split away from itself. Everything inside me went quiet as the weight of the moment settled in. There are moments when life doesn't slow down, but instead it shatters.

I lifted her into my arms, whispering, *"Mom, I love you,"* over and over, while begging God to keep her with us. I held her the way a child holds a mother when the roles reverse without warning, trying to steady her even as everything inside me was shaking. I wasn't thinking about what to do next; I was simply moving on instinct and love, refusing to believe that this was how her story would end.

An ambulance came, followed by an emergency helicopter. The deafening noise of the blades cutting through the air felt violent against the silence that had just lived in that room. They flew her out, rushed her where I could not follow fast enough. I stood there shaking, knowing only one thing for certain, that whatever came next would change us forever.

That was the first time I truly understood how thin the line between life and death really is.

I stood in a hospital room watching my mother fight for her life while doctors told us she might only have minutes left due to a brain bleed. The air felt heavy as my family gathered at her bedside, not praying for outcomes, not asking for explanations, but begging for peace. For healing. I prayed for her suffering to end, one way or another. We braced ourselves for the possibility that we were about to say goodbye.

What happened next was something none of us expected.

The outcome the doctors had prepared us for never came. Her body began to respond, slowly stabilizing in ways they could not easily explain. What had looked like the final moments of her life shifted into something none of us had dared to hope for.

She is alive today, still carrying scars from that night and still battling the long shadow of her past and addiction.

That moment carved something permanent into me. Watching her fight for her life changed the way I understood resilience. I had seen what it looked like to keep fighting when everything suggested it was time to stop, and that knowledge stayed with me long after the hospital room faded into memory.

That moment became my foundation.

My instinct to protect did not lead me to comfort; it led me to the military. I was done being powerless. I chose structure over chaos, discipline over destruction, and service over silence. In many ways, I was running away from the life I came from, determined not to repeat it.

The military was hard, but it was not harder than the life I had already survived. I had been trained by trauma long before I wore a uniform. I knew how to endure discomfort, how to stay alert, how to keep moving when quitting felt easier. The difference was that this time, the hardship had purpose. The rules were clear. The expectations were defined. Strength was built intentionally, not out of necessity alone.

That realization reshaped my identity.

Today, I don't shy away from difficulty. I seek it. Ultra-marathon running. Bodybuilding competitions. Pushing my body past perceived limits. This is how I channel what was once fear into something measurable, achievable, and earned.

Where pain once dictated my direction, challenge now fuels my growth. I no longer survive difficulty; I harness it. I turn pressure into progress, discipline into mastery, and resilience into achievement.

The life I was given was brutal. The life I am building is intentional. And every mile run, every weight lifted, every finish line crossed is proof that hardship does not have to break you; it can become the very thing that defines your strength.

I eventually came to understand that care itself is a form of strength. Gentleness is not weakness, and creating calm in a chaotic world can be its own kind of resistance.

As I grew older, the fear that once lived in my body slowly transformed. At first, it became anger, and over time, that anger sharpened into determination—determination to protect, to build safety, and to make sure the people around me felt seen and cared for.

Trauma had taught me to read a room before I ever made eye contact. I could feel shifts in energy before words were spoken. Instead of allowing that awareness to harden into bitterness, I began to turn it toward leadership and care.

In time, beauty found its way back into my life.

Today, I have been in the beauty industry for nearly two decades, but hair was never simply a profession to me. It is something I was pulled toward long before I had words for it. Even before I understood that what I was really seeking was connection, restoration, and a way to care for others in this world.

I began doing hair at a young age, guided by instinct more than intention. Over time, what started as a skill became a language. A quiet exchange between two people. A way to rebuild confidence when life had stripped it away. Through years of hands-on experience, continued education, and work that spanned luxury salons, runways, editorial spaces, and high-pressure training environments, my relationship with hair deepened not just technically, but emotionally. Hair became the place where artistry and humanity met.

Beauty became the way I learned to make people feel safe. In the salon chair, in the ritual of transformation, people exhale. In the quiet rhythm of the work—washing, cutting, styling—they soften in ways that conversation alone rarely allows. For a moment, people can simply sit, breathe, and feel cared for. They can feel whole, even briefly. In those moments, I saw what healing could look like when it is quiet and intentional.

This is why my craft is sacred.

Hair is never just hair. It is part of a person's identity and dignity. When I pour everything into my God-given craft, it is because I know what it feels like to create a home I feel safe in. Not to escape life, but to survive it and thrive in it.

Sometimes beauty is born in the darkest rooms, in the quiet act of caring for someone when they need it most. I chose this career out of love. For me it's impactful to reach people far beyond appearance. Hair reflects how we see ourselves and how safe we feel being seen by others. When someone sits in my chair, they are not simply trusting me with their hair; they are trusting me with their vulnerability, their story, and sometimes their healing. That kind of trust demands presence, respect, and care.

At a certain point, I created a brand intentionally. **Shear Studios** was born from that understanding. It was created as a space where beauty is intentional, elevated, and rooted in humanity. A place where guests feel held, where professionals are supported and challenged to grow, and where excellence is expected without sacrificing compassion. Every service is guided by integrity, education, and deep respect for individuality, hair health, and lived experience.

I carry a healthy obsession with growth. With pushing limits. With helping others rise. Because I have seen what happens when someone fights to live and what becomes possible when they refuse to give up.

This chapter is not written to glorify pain, but to honor survival. To prove that beauty can be born in darkness. That purpose can rise from terror. That miracles exist, and responsibility follows them.

ABOUT THE AUTHOR

Sherrie Anderson is an entrepreneur, author, and industry leader recognized for her impact in the luxury beauty and wellness space. She is the Founder and Owner of Shear Studios, an award-winning destination salon in Chesterfield, Missouri, known for advanced hair design, custom color, extensions, treatments, and elevated skincare experiences. A U.S. Air Force veteran, Sherrie brings discipline, resilience, and visionary leadership to her business, building a culture rooted in excellence, education, and high performance.

An award-winning stylist and sought-after runway hair leader, she has collaborated with designers, producers, and creative teams to execute editorial and fashion-forward work at the highest level. Equally passionate about mentorship, Sherrie invests deeply in developing the next generation of beauty professionals through structured training and leadership development.

Beyond her professional accomplishments, Sherrie is a devoted mother of two and happily married. Her Christian faith anchors her life and leadership, shaping her commitment to integrity, service, and uplifting others. Through her writing and work, she draws from a personal journey marked by perseverance and purpose, inspiring readers to find strength, beauty, and transformation even in life's most challenging seasons.

Building Strength From My Scars

by Gillian Hughes

Sometimes the universe doesn't whisper. Sometimes it drops a truth in your lap so violently that you can't ignore it.

For me, that moment came one ordinary afternoon when I clicked a mouse, woke a computer screen, and watched my entire life split open.

That was the day I chose myself.

I grew up in the snowy suburbs of Ontario, Canada, a quiet, freckled rule-follower who wanted desperately to fit in and equally desperately to stand out. My parents were conservative British immigrants who believed in aiming only as high as you could safely land. I believed in something bigger: a life I didn't yet have the language to describe.

The first time I picked up a women's fitness magazine in high school, something shifted. Those strong, vibrant athletes felt like a doorway into a world where I didn't have to shrink. Long before social media, those pages became my secret window into possibility.

While my peers lingered in the high school cafeteria over lunch hour, I slipped into the empty weight room. It became my sanctuary. The clank of weights and the quiet focus of lifting gave me a sense of control I hadn't experienced anywhere else. In that room, there were no rumors, no expectations about how a girl should look or behave. There was only the simple, honest work of becoming stronger.

Lifting weights made me feel powerful in a way I didn't yet have words for. Each small improvement felt like proof that I was capable of shaping my own future. It wasn't just about physical strength; it was about discovering that I had the ability to build something within myself that no one else could take away.

But the more I sculpted my body into a strong physique, the more the outside world had its opinions about it. Rumors spread. My younger brother, three years my junior, was harassed by his peers because of the attention that I received. Instead of defending me, he pulled away, and a wedge grew between us. By senior year, I was counting down the days until I could leave a place that didn't feel safe and didn't feel like home.

After high school, I went to nursing school, not because it was my dream, but because it sounded more respectable to my family than sports medicine, the field that would have kept me closer to the world I loved.

Four years later, I graduated with a bachelor's degree in nursing. To me, that degree felt like something more than a career. It felt like a ticket to explore the world. A new beginning.

Healthcare offered endless opportunities in the United States, and I knew I could pursue my passion for fitness there as well. In my mind, crossing the border meant the chance to reinvent myself and finally become the person I had always imagined I could be.

But even with determination and purpose, I wasn't brave enough to make that bold move alone.

Before graduation, I had become involved with a complicated young man. He was two years older, from a wealthy family, and intensely intellectual. A math scholar, he would stay up until dawn scribbling numbers and symbols across huge dry-erase boards filled with formulas that looked like another language entirely.

At first, his intensity felt like passion. Over time, it became control.

His expectations governed my behavior and choices. Slowly, I began distancing myself from friends under his influence. I remember knowing in my heart that it was wrong to change myself for someone, yet pieces of me quietly disappeared inside that relationship. I started questioning my instincts and doubting my ability to make decisions without his approval.

When he was accepted into a master's program in the United States, I followed. I crossed the border into Florida with one suitcase, five hundred dollars in my bank account, and a head full of determination that my family and friends didn't quite understand. Even though I moved with someone who was supposed to love me, I had never felt more alone.

Once we settled in Florida, doubts crept in. I loved my nursing job and the independence it gave me, but I couldn't ignore the growing unease in my relationship.

We shared bills. We talked about marriage. But the thought of marrying him filled me with panic. Still, I stayed. Part of me convinced myself that his possessiveness was love. Another part feared I might fail if I tried to build a life in America on my own. I wondered if things were really "bad enough" to justify leaving. Months passed while I slowly stopped trusting myself. Then one afternoon, everything changed.

I left work early to print documents my employer needed. When I walked into our apartment office, I noticed his computer had been left on. Rather than start up my own laptop, I nudged the mouse to wake the screen.

What appeared before me was an email thread. Dozens of messages between him and another woman. They were making plans to reconnect and meet in our apartment while I was home in Canada for Christmas. From the tone of the emails, it was clear this relationship had existed long before we even left Canada.

In the messages he sent her, he described his life in Florida as if he were living there alone. Suntanned selfies. Stories of adventures in the Sunshine State. What he didn't mention was *me*.

He didn't mention the girlfriend of two years who had moved to Florida with him—the woman he had spoken about marrying. Standing there in front of the screen, my heart shattered. But beneath the shock was something unexpected. Relief.

The control and emotional manipulation I had been living under had slowly chipped away at my spirit. I had wanted to leave, but couldn't find the courage. Now I had a reason. I packed my belongings quietly during the day while he was at class. I found a small apartment, bought a blow-up mattress to sleep on, and used a bicycle as my main form of transportation.

I left behind most of my possessions. But I kept something far more important. My freedom.

The years that followed were not a straight climb upward but a slow journey back to myself. I worked extra shifts at the hospital so I could eventually afford a car. I built friendships with coworkers.

I reconnected with the fitness community that had once given me so much confidence. I trained. I modeled. I took risks that the frightened twenty-one-year-old on the air mattress could never have imagined.

Eventually, I met another nurse who shared my love of bodybuilding and fitness. We married, started a family, and began building a life together. For a while, everything seemed to be unfolding exactly as I had once dreamed.

Then in 2010, life changed again. My father was diagnosed with terminal brain cancer. At the same time, my husband's father became ill and passed away from heart failure. In the middle of all of that grief, we discovered we were pregnant with our second child. Joy and sorrow collided in ways I wasn't prepared for.

Pregnancy, loss, and exhaustion pulled me further away from the healthy habits that had once anchored me. My body felt foreign after pregnancy, childbirth, and so much sorrow. Life was heavy, and again I felt alone. Once my babies were asleep each night, I turned to junk food and alcohol, drinking glass after glass of wine to dull the pain and attempt to sleep. My marriage was on the verge of collapse, and I didn't recognize the person in the mirror.

I felt ashamed and too discouraged to even walk into a gym again—the very place that had once made me feel alive. Then I remembered that moment years earlier when I chose myself and walked away from a life that was breaking me. This time, the decision was even clearer. I wasn't just choosing myself. I was choosing my children.

I began slowly. Five pounds lost became twenty. Strength returned to my body and, just as importantly, to my mind. As my health improved, so did my confidence. I began sharing pieces of my journey online, and I realized something powerful: there were countless other women walking the same path.

Women who felt lost in motherhood. Women who had forgotten their own goals. Women who believed they had to shrink in order to care for everyone else. Women who felt invisible and alone. I wanted to change that narrative.

At first, it started in small ways. I began sharing my workouts, the changes I was making in my habits, and the lessons I was learning about rebuilding confidence after motherhood and loss. I wasn't trying to build a business at the time. I was simply sharing honestly about what I was experiencing.

Some days that meant posting a quick workout from my home gym. Other days, it meant talking openly about how hard it was to start again after feeling like I had lost myself. I shared the messy parts—the days when motivation was low, the moments when I wondered if I could really rebuild my strength while raising children and managing everything else life demanded.

But something unexpected happened. Women began reaching out. They told me they felt the same way I once had, tired, disconnected from their bodies, unsure if they could ever feel strong or confident again. Many of them had spent years putting themselves last. Their messages weren't asking for perfection. They were asking for guidance from someone who understood what it felt like to start over.

The more conversations I had, the more I realized that my story wasn't just about me. It was about the thousands of women who had quietly put themselves last for years.

That's when my small coaching business began to grow. I created a program called *Momshell Method Fitness*, designed to help mothers reclaim their strength without sacrificing family life or their sense of self.

At first, it was just a handful of women. We trained together, shared goals, and celebrated the smallest victories—an extra push-up, a stronger squat, the confidence to walk back into a gym after years away. I began creating simple programs that focused not just on appearance, but on strength, energy, and confidence.

What surprised me most was how quickly the community grew. Women told their friends. Mothers invited other mothers. The conversations expanded beyond workouts into something deeper: how to prioritize your health without sacrificing your family, how to reclaim time for yourself without guilt, and how to remember that you matter too.

Eventually, I took a leap of faith and left my nursing career to focus entirely on fitness coaching. Leaving nursing was not an easy decision. It had been my identity for years, and the career that first gave me the independence to build a life in America. But the more women I helped through coaching, the clearer it became that this work was where I felt most aligned.

I saw women rediscover confidence they thought they had lost forever. I watched mothers stand taller, move stronger, and speak about themselves with pride instead of doubt. The impact went far beyond physical change. It was about helping women reconnect with their own power.

As the community grew, so did the conversations we were having. Women weren't just asking about workouts—they were asking about confidence, balance, motherhood, relationships, and how to rebuild their sense of identity after years of putting themselves last.

In 2024, that desire for deeper conversations led to another unexpected opportunity. Together with a close friend and fellow coach from Momshell Method, we launched the *Bikinis After Babies Podcast*. What began as a simple passion project quickly grew into a space where women from around the world could hear honest conversations about strength, motherhood, and the courage it takes to pursue their own goals while raising a family.

Helping women rediscover themselves has become my purpose.

But, along the way, I also had to confront another truth: my marriage had reached its end. With the confidence I had rebuilt in myself, I found the courage to walk away and begin again as a single mother. It was one of the hardest choices I have ever made. But it was also one of the most empowering.

Because what I learned through every chapter of my story is this: Strength isn't just about physical transformation. It's about learning to trust yourself. It's about believing that you are capable, worthy, and resilient enough to rebuild your life when everything feels broken.

Transformation rarely happens in one dramatic moment. It happens in small decisions made over and over again. Choosing to show up for yourself when it would be easier not to. Choosing to believe that your life can still evolve, even after heartbreak, grief, or divorce.

Strength is not about never struggling. It's about learning that you can move through struggle without losing yourself. Every time I chose to stand back up, to start again, to believe that something better was possible, I was building the life I now live.

Today, my mission is to share that message with other women.

You don't have to shrink.

You don't have to settle.

And you don't have to lose yourself while caring for everyone else. The power to rebuild your life has always been inside you. You can only find it if you choose yourself first.

ABOUT THE AUTHOR

Gillian Hughes is an entrepreneur, online health and fitness coach, podcast host, and IFBB Bikini Professional dedicated to helping women build strong, confident bodies through sustainable lifestyle change. She holds a Bachelor of Science degree from McMaster University in Hamilton, Canada, and has coached over 1,000 women worldwide, guiding them toward transformative results in strength, body composition, and overall well-being.

With a passion for empowering women- especially mothers navigating the demands of family life- Gillian combines science-based strategy with real-world experience to help clients create lasting habits and achieve goals they once thought were out of reach. Her approach blends performance-driven training, mindset development, and practical nutrition to support women at every stage of their fitness journey.

Originally from London, Canada, Gillian now resides in St. Louis, Missouri, in a big blended family with her husband Bryan and their combined five children. She hosts the podcast "Bikinis After Babies", where she shares candid conversations and expert insights on fitness, motherhood, and personal growth. Through her work, Gillian continues to inspire women to pursue their strongest selves, inside and out.

How The Storm Taught Me To Love

by Caroline Jamry

I Didn't Break, I Melted

Transformation never comes politely. It doesn't knock. It doesn't wait. It arrives like a storm—ripping through the life you've carefully crafted and leaving you blinking in the wreckage, wondering who you are now that everything familiar has fallen apart.

My storm arrived at thirty-six.

I had been a wife for seven years of my thirteen-year relationship, and when that ended, so did the version of myself I had spent my entire adult life performing. The achiever, the planner, the perfectionist who followed the rules. I did everything *right:* good school, good job, marriage, child, stability.

But life has a way of showing you exactly where you've been asleep.

When my marriage dissolved, the collapse wasn't just external—it was internal. The identity I had neatly assembled cracked open, and what spilled out was the truth: I had been living my life to please what society expected of me, and in the process, I grew to dislike parts of myself to fit in. The result? I attracted people into my life who mirrored the way that I felt about myself. I was hard on myself, and so I attracted a partner who criticized me instead of lifting me up.

I learned that relationships are mirrors, and that until we learn to love ourselves, we are going to keep attracting people who don't love us. Instead, they mirror back how we feel about ourselves. In my case, I was critical of myself because I hadn't yet accepted who I truly was.

Society has a way of making you feel bad about your quirks. In the process, I had disconnected myself from my own feelings, my own heart. In order to survive in the world, sometimes you have to keep your head down and push through, but in doing that, we become more like robots rather than human.

Understanding my astrology birth chart and my personality blueprint helped me accept all parts of myself, and began the journey to having unconditional love for myself, and attracting partners who mirrored that back to me. But first, I had to connect with my feminine and learn how to open my heart—to have strong boundaries but an open heart. The journey to get there took nine years.

The Ice Queen

A friend once called me *the Ice Queen.* I laughed it off at the time, but the truth stung. I had become a woman who could hold everything together—but couldn't let anything in. The girl who felt safer managing emotions than expressing them. The woman who equated vulnerability with danger.

But divorce is a brutal excavator. It digs up everything you didn't want to feel.

In the middle of my grief, confusion, and numbness, I reached out—almost randomly—to an ex-boyfriend from college who I hadn't spoken to in thirteen years. To my shock, he responded within the hour:

"You're in St. Louis? I'll be there for business next week."

The timing was unreal. Coincidental. Divine. Something in me stirred—a knowing I couldn't explain. It felt like the Universe had pulled back the sky just long enough to whisper, *Pay attention.*

It was the first time I realized that perhaps there were greater forces in the universe that I couldn't comprehend. I hadn't grown up in a household where God or spirituality were invoked often, and until that point, I got through life through pure grit, worry, and trying to control outcomes.

It was the moment I realized something bigger was happening than what my logical mind could grasp. And that moment became the first lightning bolt on my spiritual path.

The Work of Becoming

Connecting with the ex-boyfriend from college was spiritually significant, but it was not the end of my journey. Spoiler alert: we didn't work out. What followed wasn't glamorous. No swift breakthroughs. No overnight enlightenment. Just the raw, uncomfortable truth of sitting with myself—really sitting—for the first time in my adult life.

I faced my emotional detachment.
I examined my relationship patterns.
I questioned why I had chosen partners who were controlling (hint: it's because I was also controlling).
I confronted the ways I had abandoned myself to keep the peace for other people.
I unpacked the identity I had built around performing for other people's expectations.

While exploring these relationship topics, I would see online ads for something I had never heard of: Astrology birth charts. Sure, I knew my zodiac sign, but other than that, I didn't know anything about the topic.

I filled out an online birth chart calculator, and for the first time in my life, I felt seen.

Not long after that, I fell deeply, almost obsessively, into astrology. Not the surface-level horoscopes, but the ancient, intricate system that maps the psyche and the soul.

Discovering my birth chart was so validating in accepting who I truly am.

Astrology didn't just help me understand what had happened in my life.
It helped me understand *myself*. It showed me who I already was—without judgment.

My fears. My wounds. My capacity.
My tendencies. My triggers.
My purpose. My patterns.

And when I learned that Uranus—the planet of upheaval, awakening, and rebirth—was transiting my seventh house of relationships, everything clicked: My life hadn't fallen apart. It had fallen *into alignment*.

I was waking up, but it took nine years for the story to come full circle.

Nine Years of Transforming

New Year's Eve, 2016.

I was standing in my friend's apartment, phone in hand, thumb hovering over his contact. The pull was magnetic—visceral in a way that made my chest ache. I wanted to reach out. Every cell in my body was telling me to reach out.

But I didn't.

Instead, I forced myself to get ready. Showered. Did my makeup with precision. Chose an outfit that made me feel powerful. I distracted myself with shopping, with party prep, and with the careful construction of a woman who had her life together. By evening, I was dancing at Cipriani in NYC with a girlfriend, moving through the crowd like someone who didn't have an ex-boyfriend burning a hole in her consciousness.

The truth underneath?

I couldn't stop thinking about the ex-boyfriend from college, whom I had reconnected with, and who also lived in NYC. But I was hiding it—from her, from myself, from him. He had made it clear months before that he wanted to keep his distance. We weren't together. We weren't going to be together. And reaching out on New Year's Eve would have been a confession of weakness I wasn't ready to make.

So I swallowed it.

I numbed it.

I performed my way through the evening like I'd performed my way through most of my adult life—as the woman who had it all figured out. The Ice Queen. The one who didn't need anything from anyone.

As midnight struck, I was dancing, champagne in hand, surrounded by laughter and music and the collective hope of a new year. And I was completely, achingly alone.

The Pattern I Couldn't See

What I didn't understand then was that I was repeating something ancient.

The urge to reach out and the resistance against it. The feelings I was hiding. The vulnerability I was protecting like it was a wound that would never close. The way I was choosing self-protection over honest connection. The way I was abandoning myself to avoid being abandoned.

This wasn't about him.

It was about me choosing the familiar prison of emotional distance over the terrifying freedom of being truly seen.

I had built my entire identity around not needing. Around being strong enough, capable enough to handle everything alone. The feminine softness—the part of me that wanted to be chosen, that wanted to surrender, that wanted to ask for help—had been deemed too dangerous. Too risky. Too vulnerable.

So I kept her locked away.

And I kept repeating the same pattern with different men, in different contexts, with the same underlying wound: *I will protect myself by not asking for what I need.*

The years between 2016 and 2025 weren't wasted, though. They were the crucible.

The Reclamation

Five years into my healing journey, something shifted inside me. Not overnight. Not dramatically. But like the slow unfurling of something that had been compressed for decades.

I started to understand that the feminine energy I'd been taught to suppress—the softness, the receptivity, the willingness to be moved by something outside myself—wasn't weakness. It was power.

I began learning how to receive rather than chase. To soften rather than guard. To feel rather than numb. To trust rather than fear. To embody rather than perform.

And as I did, I started to attract different people. Men who were drawn to my openness rather than repelled by it. Men who wanted to show up for me, not because I had proven myself worthy through achievement, but because my presence invited them to.

I met someone who looked at me like I was the most precious thing he'd ever seen. He brought me flowers weekly. He doted on me. He supported me. He treated me with a devotion I didn't even know to hope for.

Our astrological blueprints became the lens through which I understood our connection.

When he shared his birth time early on, I pulled his chart—and suddenly his emotional rhythms, communication style, triggers, and attachment patterns came into focus. What once felt confusing made sense. The connection felt smoother, deeper, clearer.

We lasted two and a half years. Within three months, he proposed.

But after two and a half years, my soul whispered again: *It's time.*

I had to let him go. Another initiation in learning to choose myself.

The Karmic Teachers

After that engagement ended, I thought I was ready for something new. I felt open. Healed. Aligned.

The Universe had other plans.

Instead of "the one," it sent me teachers. The first was seventeen years younger—a completely different person in every external way, and yet the dynamic was identical. Same wound as with my college ex-boyfriend. Same chase. Same push-pull. Same ache of wanting to be chosen.

It was a cosmic echo. A karmic rerun.

And that's when I finally understood: *The Universe will repeat the pattern until you choose differently.*

He wasn't a mistake. He was a mirror held up to my face. He showed me where I still abandoned myself for potential, where I still confused intensity with intimacy, where I still held onto the fantasy of being chosen instead of choosing myself.

This time, I chose differently. I chose me.

The next karmic connection came with red flags I now recognized as divine protection. A man struggling with substance abuse—a relationship that could have swallowed me whole. But I didn't let it. I saw the danger, and I walked away without guilt, without the need to save him, without abandoning myself in the process.

These weren't failed relationships. They were refinements.

They weren't meant to last. They were meant to prepare me.

The Grocery Store Sign

August 2025. An ordinary Thursday evening.

I was driving to get my nails done, windows down, warm air brushing my skin, and I thought: *It would be really nice to have someone to share my life with.*

The thought was soft. Honest. Not desperate—just true.

After my nails, I debated: walk or groceries? Something told me groceries. So I drove. Green lights the entire way. A wink from the Universe.

When I walked into the store, I saw him. A man who was strikingly, unusually attractive for a grocery store on a random Thursday night. He caught my attention immediately. And in that moment, something shifted.

Maybe I should get back on the dating apps. Maybe this is a sign.

When I matched with someone the next week, I realized something uncanny: he resembled that grocery store man. More than that, he carried the energy of my college boyfriend, the one I'd reconnected with right after my divorce.

It felt like threads from my past were weaving into something new.

But this time, I showed up differently.

I joined the dating apps as my authentic self. Unapologetically spiritual. Openly into astrology. Transparent about what I wanted. I wasn't interested in debating my worldview or shrinking myself to fit someone else's comfort zone.

I was looking for resonance, not validation.

And within a week, I met someone who felt different. Grounded. Present. Emotionally available. Ready.

His birth chart told me why he sometimes went quiet. Why he processed emotions slowly. Why he needed space at certain times. Why he bonded the way he did.

Astrology gave me the keys to compassion and clarity instead of miscommunication.

And for the first time, I was in a relationship I could never have attracted before doing the inner work.

It wasn't the same man from the grocery store—I never did find him on the dating apps—but they could have been brothers.

New Year's Eve, 2025

I woke up crying.

We were technically broken up—a rupture that felt too raw, too recent, too unprocessed. And I had no plans for NYE, which made the day especially heavy. The irony wasn't lost on me: nine years ago to the day, I was dancing at Cipriani, pretending I didn't want to reach out to my ex-boyfriend from college. Now, I was home, wanting desperately to reach out to this recent connection, and terrified of what it would mean.

I tried to make plans with a girlfriend. When I got her on the phone, I broke into tears.

I told her about the breakup. I told her that he had said we should talk about it—really talk about it—and I had been resisting for two weeks: the conversation, the vulnerability, the part of me that wanted to be honest.

She listened. And then she said something that cracked me open:

"Why don't you reach out to him and tell him how you're really feeling?"

And in that moment—standing in my house on the last day of 2025—I made a choice that nine years ago me could never have made.

I chose vulnerability.

I reached out.

I was honest about my struggle processing the breakup. I leaned into the soft feminine that I had worked so hard to cultivate over the years. I let him see me—not the Ice Queen, not the woman who had it all figured out, but the real me. The one who was hurting. The one who cared. The one who was willing to be seen.

He reached out soon afterwards.

He said he'd been thinking about me too.

And we texted all of New Year's Eve. Texting was easier for me to contain my emotions, to move at a pace I could handle. But it was also real—honest, and the opposite of what I'd done nine years before.

On New Year's Day, we spoke on the phone.

The next day, we saw each other. It was a super moon. His Venus was conjunct the North Node; literally, the stars were aligned in a way that meant something. Not in a magical, problem-solving way. But in a way that said: *You're moving in the direction your soul actually wants to go.*

What Changed in Nine Years

The difference between New Year's Eve 2016 and New Year's Eve 2025 was about opening my heart to be vulnerable.

In 2016, I hid my feelings because I believed that needing someone was the same as being weak. I believed that vulnerability was a liability. I believed that the Ice Queen was my superpower.

In 2025, I acknowledged the pain instead of dancing around it. I admitted what I was feeling instead of pretending I had it handled. I let someone see me—really see me—and I didn't die from it. The world didn't collapse. I didn't lose myself.

Instead, something extraordinary happened: I found myself.

The scar I'd been carrying—the belief that I had to be emotionally invulnerable to be safe—started to transform into something else entirely.

Not because this relationship was "fixed." Not because he suddenly became what I needed him to be. But because I became someone different. Someone who could ask for what she needed. Someone who could be honest about her pain. Someone who could be soft and strong at the same time.

Someone who could choose herself *and* be open to connection.

The Storm Transformed

Do you remember the storm?

The one I described at the beginning, the one that felt like it was destroying everything I'd built?

I thought the storm was my enemy. I thought if I could just build strong enough walls, if I could just become cold enough, if I could just control enough variables, I could keep the storm from touching me.

But storms don't work that way.

And neither does life.

The storm wasn't something to resist. It was something to move through. To let it break open the parts of me that had been frozen, wash away the false self I'd been performing—and reveal what was underneath: not broken, but real.

The scar isn't the divorce. It isn't the endings or the heartbreaks or the years of self-development.

The scar is the belief I carried for decades: *I am only safe if I feel like I can control outcomes.*

And that scar is now my superpower.

Because when you reclaim your intuition and follow the signs, you find relationships that nourish. I melted the Ice Queen and walked away—not with bitterness, but with clarity. This isn't just my story. It's an invitation. Listen to your soul and to your heart. Build a life and a love aligned with your truth.

My scars didn't break me. They revealed me.

And that revelation—that becoming—is my shade of superpower.

The storm is still there. Life still moves in waves, cycles, and patterns. But I'm not hiding from it anymore. I'm not performing my way through it. I'm not abandoning myself to avoid being abandoned.

I'm moving through it as myself. Soft and strong. Vulnerable and boundaried. Open and grounded.

And that—that is what it means to finally be empowered and free.

ABOUT THE AUTHOR

Caroline Jamry is an astrologer, educator, and Karmic Pattern Guide who helps individuals transform their relationships through astrology's psychological lens. She describes the birth chart as the *original personality blueprint* — a framework that reveals emotional needs, communication styles, and the relational patterns people unconsciously repeat.

She is the founder of Personality Explained, a methodology that bridges psychology and astrology through comprehensive birth chart analysis as a foundational personality framework known for its accuracy in understanding communication and relationship dynamics.

Her work focuses on karmic connections and meaningful relationships that feel intense, confusing, or difficult to release, helping clients recognize attachment patterns and build healthier connections with partners, children, family members, and colleagues.

Using astrology as an internal compass for self-awareness and personal growth, Caroline guides individuals toward clarity, stronger communication, and deeper self-trust. Parents use her insights to better understand their children, professionals strengthen interpersonal dynamics, and individuals navigating life transitions reconnect with their inner authority.

Caroline is the author of several astrology-based books designed to help people feel seen, understood, and valued for who they truly are. She holds a B.A. in Psychology from Washington University in St. Louis and an M.A. in Social-Organizational Psychology from Teachers College, Columbia University in the City of New York.

A Path Revealed by Darkness

by Janine Lange

Am I alive? Why can't I move?

Monitors blared, and sensors bleeped. Wires were hooked up to nearly every part of my body, and someone was calling my name.

"Janine, are you with me?"

Opening my eyes and gasping for air, I replied, "Where am I? What happened to me?"

"You're in the ICU. You were admitted this morning with blood clots in both your lungs. You're lucky to be alive."

First a brain tumor, and now this. A strange dichotomy washed over me—the shock of survival tangled with a quiet, persistent worry, tugging from somewhere deep within me: Will this delay returning to nursing school?

Even in a crisis, the dream of becoming a nurse remained the ultimate goal.

———————

In contrast to many nursing students, my aspiration to pursue a career in nursing emerged later in life, inspired by an article I read in the Sunday newspaper. A local hospice organization sought volunteers to sit with terminally ill patients, giving families a chance to run errands or take time for self-care. I had firsthand experience with respite care when my father was in hospice. Their support helped my mother cope during that difficult time.

As an empty-nester, I had extra time and thought this would be a great opportunity to support struggling caregivers. I applied and, after a thorough interview and background check, was accepted, eventually being paired with several wonderful families.

The work was rewarding and inspired me to learn more about patient care. Becoming a Certified Nurse Aide was the next step. The hands-on learning—bathing, feeding, turning, comforting—offered a deeper understanding of what patients needed. While working side by side with nurses, the realization formed: *I could do that. I want to do that.* Nursing school became the goal.

At forty-five, with only a high school diploma, starting from scratch meant taking prerequisite courses to qualify for the nurse entrance exam. Despite not having been in school for more than twenty-five years, I passed all my courses with flying colors, earning the eligibility to take the exam. Diligent studying yielded a first attempt score of 94 percent, but to improve my chances for acceptance among one hundred eighty-five applicants competing for only thirty-two openings, my second attempt earned me a 97 percent score.

Waiting four weeks for an acceptance letter was torturous, and long walks with my dog became a welcome distraction. While out walking one day, I was suddenly overcome by a wave of dizziness that forced me to stop in my tracks. As I paused, it felt as though the world spun around me, much like being inside a swirling snow globe.

The episode passed quickly and was dismissed as stress.

One month later, when no letter arrived in the mail, I broke the cardinal rule and called the nursing school secretary for information on the status of my application. She shuffled a few papers until she found my file.

"We sent you a letter two weeks ago."

"I'm sorry, it never arrived. Can you tell me what it said?"

"Your first day is August 8. Be here with a white uniform and white shoes."

Thrilled beyond words, I screamed out loud. I'm going to be a nurse!

Considered a "nontraditional" student, my class consisted of twenty-eight women and four men, many younger than my three daughters. My peers were EMTs or surgical techs with prior medical experience, while my CNA background felt minimal. Still, determination outweighed intimidation, and I kept up the pace.

A second bout of dizziness was diagnosed as Vertigo. Since it had occurred only twice, it was placed on the back burner—there were bigger challenges ahead.

Things progressed nicely, and learning about nursing was exciting. Our class became a close-knit group, sharing our individual strengths and talents. Toward the end of the first semester, while sitting in the lecture hall, the professor standing at the podium became a shadowy figure shrouded in darkness. Her voice resonated in the auditorium, but her figure was lost in the haziness. Blinking didn't bring her into focus. Panic set in.

My primary care physician scheduled an appointment with a neurosurgeon for the next day, which was Friday. He performed an MRI on my brain and ran bloodwork. The results were not back before his office closed at 5:00 p.m.; thus, an agonizing weekend was spent creating doomsday scenarios. Meanwhile, my vision continued to degrade, making my world smaller.

Early Monday morning, the doctor's office called; he wanted to see me in his office as soon as possible. *This can't be good.* Projecting my scans on a small screen, he pointed to a non-cancerous tumor on my pituitary gland, pressing on the optic nerve and causing blurry vision and vertigo. The tumor was growing rapidly, necessitating immediate removal to avoid permanent vision loss. The surgery could be scheduled within a week.

My heart sank. This would definitely interfere with my well-thought-out plans. My naïve reply was, "I don't have time for that, I'm in nursing school!"

If he thought I was insane, he hid it well. "Do you want to be a blind nurse?"

Determination would not let this detour get in my way. It was December 10th, two weeks before Christmas. Finals were the next week, immediately followed by winter break for the month of January. We negotiated to have the surgery the day after my finals. My organized mind reasoned that I would have six weeks to fully recover and pick up where I left off. *That's doable.*

By the time finals arrived, my sight had worsened. Darkness dominated my world, and sunglasses were needed to make bright light tolerable. Sitting in a dimly lit room, my nursing instructor read exam questions aloud with four options for the correct answer. Struggling to concentrate, I gave her my best guesses. Only she knew whether or not the responses were correct. A little knowledge mixed with a helping of grace produced a passing grade.

Next came the Anatomy and Physiology final, far more daunting for me than the surgery. Recalling 206 bones would not be easy. Fortunately, the instructor's wife was a nurse, and he had a soft spot in his heart for nursing students. He accepted the overall semester grade in lieu of the final. The relief was overwhelming! Hopefully, the surgery would be as successful with minimal side effects and enough time to fully recuperate before returning to school. *I can do this!*

The operating room was cold, bright, and chaotic. Several nurses busied themselves setting up equipment trays, oxygen, IV supplies, dressings, etc. The commotion was disturbing. Mercifully, it didn't take long for the anesthesia to silence the noise and distinguish the lights. This time, the darkness felt safe.

The pituitary gland is located at the base of the brain behind the bridge of the nose. To access it, the surgeon temporarily shifted my nose to the side of my face. He then "resected" or cut the tumor into small pieces to remove it.

Shortly after surgery began, a spinal fluid leak required a temporary halt, and a graft from the thigh was needed. After being stabilized, the surgeon continued. Several hours passed before the tumor was fully excised, releasing pressure from the optic nerve. When the anesthesia wore off, I was relieved to find my eyesight had returned to normal. *Okay, maybe this won't be so bad after all.*

Seven days later, the doctor released me, but something didn't feel right. He dismissed my symptoms as being typical after surgery of this magnitude. Returning home to my mother's nearby house felt safer than traveling over an hour to school. My instincts were correct.

At 5 a.m., my sleep was abruptly interrupted by sharp, stabbing pains in my chest. Unable to take a breath, my lungs felt like they were filled with cement. My mother was leaving for work. Feeble attempts to call out to her failed. As she opened the front door to leave, throwing my pillow down the stairs in hopes that she would see it seemed the only viable option. Just as she was closing the door, she caught sight of the pillow in the corner of her eye. The last thing I remember before losing consciousness was whispering, "Call 911."

Seven days in the ICU and another week in the hospital left less than three weeks to rebuild my strength before school started again. Still recuperating from the blood clots, my lungs were operating at only 50 percent. It was difficult to walk and breathe at the same time without stopping every hundred feet. The Director of Nursing witnessed this and stopped me before returning to class.

"I'm sorry, you cannot attend school in this condition. You're a liability. You'll have to drop out and try coming back next year."

Mustering as much courage and breath as I could, I replied, "Withdrawing from the program is not an option. At forty-five, this is my one shot at becoming a nurse. There is no next year for me."

My mind raced to produce a workable compromise. We could schedule less strenuous clinical rotations at the beginning of the semester and save the twelve-hour hospital rounds for later in the year. She reluctantly agreed to the arrangement with the caveat that one slip-up would result in immediate dismissal. It was a much-needed glimmer of hope. I promised it would be done, but had no idea how to execute the plan.

My heart and soul were ready to return to school, but my body wouldn't cooperate. Unfortunately, no one explained the residual effects of living without a pituitary gland. Temperature regulation was impaired. Steroid use to reduce swelling in the brain caused insomnia, which led to fatigue. Simple decision-making skills, such as deciding what to eat, became overwhelming and induced panic. Putting my symptoms aside, I forged ahead.

During a surgical rotation, the face mask and tight gloves caused me to overheat, sending me running out of the operating room.

"What's wrong with your friend? Can't she handle blood and guts?" the surgeon asked my classmate.

"No, she's tough as nails and can handle a lot. She's recovering from brain surgery."

The surgeon found me lying face down on the floor in the supply room, trying to cool down. "I heard you had your pituitary removed. Did anyone tell you what to expect after surgery?"

"No. I'm just trying to make it from one day to the next without passing out."

The surgeon was understanding and kind enough to spend over an hour telling me why my body wasn't functioning properly, something my own doctor failed to do. He explained that the pituitary is the "Master Gland" which regulates temperature, metabolism, growth, thyroid activity, water and sodium balance, and stress management. His compassion offered the first real understanding of why my body felt foreign. It all started to make sense.

"Thank you, that explains a lot. I thought I was dying."

"No, it's just your body adjusting to the hormonal changes. It may take up to a year or more until you reach normal function again. Nursing school is extremely demanding under the best conditions. I honestly don't know how you're doing it."

"That's how badly I want to be a nurse."

My endocrinologist created a medication regimen to compensate for the lack of hormonal regulation in my body. After several months of dosing trial and error attempts, we finally got it right, and I started feeling human again.

Maintaining my grades wasn't easy, given my impaired ability to concentrate. Sleep eluded me, and bargaining with the clock became a habit. *"It's 2 a.m., if I fall asleep right now, three hours will be enough to get me through the day."*

My fellow students stepped up to the plate to help me. They recorded lectures, cooked meals, and did my laundry. They drove me to and from school and helped me study. One classmate in particular offered to spend the night on my couch due to my recurring fear of developing another blood clot in my sleep. Her support was a blessing.

Being a visual learner, my apartment walls were littered with multi-colored posters depicting body systems, medication uses, side effects, and medical interventions. Associating various subjects with specific colors made it easier to remember the course material when taking exams. Listening to audio lessons during sleepless nights helped with memorization.

The final semester arrived along with the twelve-hour clinical rotations. It was all that stood between me and my goal to become a Registered Nurse. The long hospital shifts required endurance, but I had a new perspective now, one earned through pain, fear, and the willingness to overcome adversity to attain my dream.

As a novice student nurse, apprehension in my new role slowly gave way to confidence. From my experiences, I was able to meet people where they were. My impaired eyesight taught me to see my patients with a clear vision; as people with feelings who need compassion, have their hand held, or be told it's okay to cry. I understood the stress of trying to hold on to the slightest bit of control when everything is out of your hands, and I gave my patients grace when they became agitated or upset. Listening to their needs, rather than quickly administering medications and moving on, helped ease their anxiety. I may have moved more slowly, but the extra time was well spent.

When May came, I stood on the stage with my graduating class of nurses. After our pinning ceremony, the director of nursing sought me out. Her words validated my journey.

"I'm sure glad you didn't listen to me. You'll make a fine nurse," she told me.

"Thank you, Mavis. That means a lot to me."

I was a hospice nurse for over eight years. It was an honor and a privilege to provide support to many patients and their families during a difficult time in their lives, realizing this gift needed to be shared with other aspiring nurses. I earned my master's degree, became the Director of Nursing Education, and wrote and taught courses to nurses and nurse aides on providing hospice care. I also taught seminary students who ministered to the spiritual needs of dying patients in their congregations. The goal was always the same: help them see the person beyond the illness.

No textbook or nursing course can teach empathy, compassion, or understanding. These lessons are learned through experiences that touch the core of our being, the ones that leave an indelible mark on our lives.

My trials redefined not only my nursing practice, but my outlook on life. Providing care to others isn't just a career; it exemplifies who I am as a person.

Giving up never occurred to me. I fought for my life to emerge from the darkness and travel the path I was destined to take. The battle won was well worth the fight.

More significantly, my personal experience as a patient—enduring pain, fear, and uncertainty—profoundly influenced and reshaped the philosophy of my nursing practice. Compassion and understanding became the basis of my holistic approach to treating patients' physical, mental, and emotional needs.

Graduating from nursing school happened not in spite of my illness, but because of it. Many lessons were learned. Remember:

A goal without a plan is just a dream.

When the path is blocked, one must pivot and renegotiate the roadmap.

Determination can override physical impairments.

ABOUT THE AUTHOR

Janine Lange is an award-winning, best-selling author and Master's-prepared nurse whose career has been defined by a passion for education, leadership, and elevating the nursing profession. With over 20 years of experience guiding new and seasoned nurses, she has developed a reputation for clear, compassionate teaching and innovative approaches to professional growth.

Her first published book on Nursing Orientation—an award-winning resource that earned national recognition for its practical insight and impact on nursing development—established her as both an educator and a respected voice in the field.

Building on her lifelong love of history and storytelling, Janine now brings her talents to the world of Historical Fiction. Her novels blend thorough research with deep human narratives, offering readers stories that feel both intimate and timeless.

Through richly drawn characters and evocative settings, she explores the resilience of family bonds, the lessons of the past, and the enduring power of love to carry people through the most challenging moments.

Whether writing to educate or to inspire, Janine's work reflects her belief in the strength of individuals and the beauty of shared stories.

The Dollhouse Project

by Tracie C. Hulbert

My husband Daniel and I had just recently purchased my childhood home from my parents. We had welcomed our fourth baby after I spent the last seven months of my pregnancy on complete bed rest. At the same time, I stepped away from the nonprofit world I had spent the last eight or so years of my life building—often as an unpaid volunteer—protecting the integrity of our mission. My passion was to meet people where they were, doing the very best that we possibly could for them. We were a safe place, a kind ear, a true partner to help, and maybe for the first time, an ear to really listen, understand, and not judge.

The days were tough, but I really felt like I was made for it. I have always seen things for exactly what they are, and more importantly, I view the world like a puzzle. Except I only see the missing pieces.

I was connected to some pretty amazing people who would ask me to come speak—not because I had a title, but because I had seen real change. I had watched ordinary people do extraordinary things when they understood how to organize their time, their talent, and their treasure.

When people asked how any of this worked, I tried to explain that the networks we built were more than names stored in a phone. They were lifelines. The systems weren't corporate structures or organizational charts; they were bridges connecting people who knew how to help with people who needed it.

Over time, I watched something remarkable happen. When generosity was organized, and people trusted one another, it became its own kind of infrastructure. Through the relationships we had built, we could often step in quickly when a family was struggling. Groceries could be delivered, rent could be covered for the month, childcare could be arranged, and someone could make the phone calls that opened the door to a new opportunity.

What still amazes me is how quickly it could happen. In many cases, a family's most immediate needs could be met within twenty-four hours. There were no waiting lists, no applications, and no funding streams to navigate or grants to write. Just people who trusted one another and knew how to move when someone needed help.

And it wasn't limited to one neighborhood or even one city. The network stretched across more than seven hundred miles, connecting different communities and zip codes.

Even now, that humbles me.

Because what it showed me is this: the real currency has never just been money. It's a relationship. It's credibility. It's leadership. It's the willingness to pick up the phone and say, "We have a need," and know someone on the other end will say, "I'm in."

It was incredible. Honestly, that's a story all its own.

But what moved me the most wasn't the speed. It wasn't even the scale.

After sharing what I knew in hopes it would help others create the same impact and help more families, I was asked to be a board ambassador for a local Chamber of Commerce. It was an honor—and I declined. The Executive Director asked why I turned them down, so I explained that, as much as I would love to help, I couldn't justify having my little one stay with someone else, just so I could go volunteer. She smiled and said, "Bring him. We love babies, and I'll help."

I said, "I can't do that. Those business owners don't want to hear my kid crying."

Then she said the magic words: "We can't say we support women in business and then not support the *whole* woman. You're fantastic. If they don't like it, they don't have to be here."

That was an *aha* moment. The entire drive home, I sat with the realization that we are far more capable than we've been led to believe. It was the first time someone didn't just give me a seat at a table I didn't have to build—she removed the roadblocks and pulled the chair out for me.

My baby went to those meetings and many other organizations with me for years, and still does to this day. In a pumpkin seat, on a play mat, on my hip, crying, quiet, and everything in between. And you know what? We created a lot of really beautiful things that helped and protected a lot of families. Motherhood didn't pause the mission; it came with it.

When I look back, I'm proud of how many people we've been able to help—mostly women and children. Most did absolutely nothing wrong. They worked hard and simply needed a hand *up*, not a handout. And I'd constantly be asked: how did we pull it off? And more importantly, how do we keep these women from ending up in the same place?

There was only one reason—that taboo little word: ***money.***

Money would have made a whole lot of things a whole lot easier. In our own home, and in every home I know. Financial stress hurts everyone. When everything costs money, it becomes harder to ask for help, and uncertainty starts to feel like personal failure instead of a shared reality. So people suffer in silence—embarrassed and alone.

But here's the truth no one says out loud: Silence around money isn't accidental. It's cultural. It's inherited. For women especially, the taboo runs deeper. We were encouraged to be grateful rather than informed, trusting rather than strategic, supported rather than independent. We were told someone else would handle it. Or that wanting more was "too much." Or that talking about money was tacky.

So many women became experts at stretching, sacrificing, and surviving...
but not owning, investing, and leading. The conversation has to change.

Nine-to-five sounds cute. But I'd bet this framework was created when there was a wife at home—raising children, cooking and cleaning—while the husband went to work. Why nine to five? Why are financial institutions only open while everyone who needs them is working?

Kids are in school from six to two, seven to three, and nine to four. Trust me—I know. We have four, and we both work. Sometimes we work two or three jobs, all while managing household chores, finances, sports, and holidays. You know how it is. Even having time to read this book is a miracle.

So how do I make my own schedule, honor my gifts, help others, and still be *me*?

It started with an open door.

Heather, with her crystal blue eyes and big, beautiful smile, crossed my social media feed. She was walking around a lake in the middle of the day, sun on her face, talking about a family she had just helped. She shared that she was interviewing to teach others how to do the same.

I had known Heather for almost ten years. She was smart, hard-working, sweet, and always positive. She had even held my baby for me at meetings once or twice. She was sharing about her company—an opportunity that was 100 percent virtual and 100 percent commission-based.

I began to research everything about it. And I mean *everything*. The culture seemed phenomenal. I connected with their values and their origin story. They were people just like me, my family, and the people I love.

After a couple of weeks, I reached out to Heather. I told her, "I want to do this—if you'll have me." That decision changed my life.

Funny thing—when you surround yourself with kind, brilliant, generous people, you meet more of them. You bounce ideas. Build systems. Learn what works and what doesn't. You see how grassroots efforts spread a mission when there's never enough money and never enough volunteers—because the system burns them out.

Then one day you blink and ask: "What do I do with twenty years of this so-called *useless knowledge?* What is my purpose?"

I wanted to do what I've always done—on my schedule—and be wildly successful, creating a beautiful legacy for my babies.

I wanted to bring gifted, wildly brilliant women and men with me. I watched my sweet husband work days, nights, travel endlessly, chase certifications, and pursue education to give our family the best. That was only possible because I could be home with our children—pivoting my schedule, working early mornings and late nights, filling every nook and cranny of my day. That's how the nonprofits were built.

I wanted to reinvent that wheel—for everyone.

A model that worked in the background while people lived their lives. A business that was virtual, adaptable, and human. And yes—I want to work hard, get a lot done, and never feel like I'm working.

That's how **The Dollhouse Project** was born.

A model rooted in generosity, dignity, and being good humans. When people feel supported, they show up stronger. When they're empowered, they contribute more. And when people realize they can shape the opportunity around what they *need*, they become unstoppable.

An army of bold, protective women and men who genuinely want to serve the greater good.

I didn't build The Dollhouse Project for headlines or hype. I built it for kitchens where bills are opened quietly. For parents who are doing the math twice before saying yes. For the moments when women whisper their fears about money.

What if instead of hoarding knowledge, we shared it? What if people offered their time, talents, skills, passions, and care—not out of obligation, but because they understood that helping others strengthens everyone?

We created a Volunteer Army—free to anyone who wants to learn and plug in. Financial literacy. Meal prep. Budgeting. Health and wellness coaches. Sustainable living experts. Mental health advocates. Book clubs.

We all need help. And no one should be afraid to ask for it—or unsure if they can trust the person offering it. I will never ask anyone on my team to choose this over the most important things in their lives. We adapt. We pivot. It's not that serious.

Instead of building walls, we open rooms—exactly as needed, case by case.

The Dollhouse Project is my blueprint for a financially safe empire for women and young families: bold, intentional, protective, and beautiful. Because when women are financially empowered, the foundation of our communities changes, and the world changes with them.

Women need to make more money, but there aren't enough hours. Who watches the kids? How much is a sitter? Does it even make sense once the math is done?

I wanted to build something that didn't just teach families about money, but armed them with tools to grow their finances. A place where wealth wasn't intimidating. Where conversations about assets and protection felt as normal as talking about careers or relationships.

No franchise fees. No overhead beyond a cell phone. Minimal investment. A business launch designed specifically for *them*. No smoke and mirrors. If you believe in yourself and take my hand, I'm running with you.

That's the Dollhouse—separate rooms addressing individual goals and futures. A space where everyone has a seat at the table. Can't afford to invest yet? We'll help you get there. Don't understand? We'll empower you.

This isn't about dollars. It's about dignity. Options. The future.

I made a bold logo with hot pink and red because I can. Hot pink is unapologetic femininity reclaimed. Red is power, urgency, fire. This is the face of the new financial landscape—everyday people living real lives, sharing what they know so maybe life gets a little easier than the "just work more" mentality.

You can be powerful, brilliant, and full of life—and have fun doing it.

I want to shape a culture, a movement built on bold care, shared power, and the belief that no one needs fixing. We can build futures together and leave the table bigger than we found it. Because, for as long as I can remember, money felt like a different world for women. Why did Meme keep her cash in a coffee can on top of the cabinets? We're taught to make money—but never how to make it work for us.

We've watched people carry entire worlds on their backs—mothers, fathers, daughters, sons, partners—brilliant individuals holding families, careers, and dreams all at once. Too often, they did it without the financial protection they deserved, not for lack of ambition, but for lack of access, knowledge, or a safe place to learn. And still, they showed up, persisted, and carried their brilliance into spaces that weren't built for them.

Families deserve power, protection, and the tools to thrive together. This is why The Dollhouse Project exists: for households calculating every decision, for whispered fears about money no one should face alone. Together—equipped, unafraid, and united—we can transform the weight of the world into a network of support, strength, and hope.

This is that place. A home. A place to breathe, to plan, to dream bigger than you thought possible. A place to rise, to grow, to build, and to carry your loved ones forward with confidence and dignity.

Welcome to The Dollhouse Project.

Welcome home.

ABOUT THE AUTHOR

Tracie C. Hulbert is an entrepreneur, financial educator, and visionary leader committed to protecting families and empowering women to build financially secure futures. With a foundation rooted in nonprofit leadership and grassroots community mobilization, she spent nearly two decades building expansive service networks that met urgent family needs—often within twenty-four hours and without grant funding or government support. Her work has consistently centered on dignity, access, and sustainable impact.

After transitioning into the financial services industry, Tracie combined her passion for advocacy with strategic financial education, creating a model that equips families not only to navigate crisis—but to prevent it. She is the founder of The Dollhouse Project, a bold, community-driven initiative designed to develop leaders, expand financial literacy, and create scalable, flexible income opportunities—particularly for women balancing career and family.

Known for her unapologetic authenticity and disciplined mentorship, Tracie has helped build high-performing teams across multiple states, empowering everyday individuals to increase income, strengthen leadership capacity, and establish generational stability.

Through her writing and leadership, she champions financial empowerment as a form of protection—because when women gain clarity, confidence, and control over money, families and communities are transformed.

Terminally Alive

by Melissa Burns

For nearly two decades, I had been slowly disappearing—losing parts of myself until there was barely anything recognizable left. I vanished, piece by piece, into the noise and the neglect. I had no choice but to sit there and let it happen.

I felt like a scared child who had run into the woods and taken shelter in a rotting, forgotten cabin. I was hiding—angry, hurt, and alone. And then, seemingly out of nowhere, she showed up. It was January 6, 2020. The day of my formal diagnosis.

She found me in that place. She sat down in the dust and silence with me, and reached out her hand—not to fix me, but to acknowledge that I had been broken. I'd been keeping the shattered fragments of who I used to be in a box, just in case some miracle ever allowed me to be whole again.

For the first time in years, I wasn't afraid to take someone's hand. I still questioned whether she really believed me. That fear doesn't vanish overnight. But she pulled me out of the loneliest place I have ever been in my life.

To someone who's never lived it, this might all sound dramatic. But if you've ever been there—lost in your own body, abandoned by medicine, dismissed by people who were supposed to help; you know exactly what I mean.

My twenty-plus years of medical chaos suddenly had a name: Ehlers-Danlos Syndrome.

Per the Ehlers-Danlos Society website: "The Ehlers-Danlos syndromes (EDS) are a group of thirteen heritable connective tissue disorders. The conditions are caused by genetic changes that affect connective tissue. Each type of EDS has its own set of features with distinct diagnostic criteria. Some features are seen across all types of EDS, including joint hypermobility, skin hyperextensibility, and tissue fragility."

Every system in your body is comprised of connective tissue, meaning every system in your body has the opportunity to suffer a variety of degrees of complication.

To be fair, I had already done a lot of research on Ehlers-Danlos Syndrome by the time I reached that point. I suspected it was the root of everything. Countless nights were spent awake, scouring the internet for similarities—symptoms, patient stories, anything that felt familiar. I searched every corner of Google. I joined Facebook groups filled with people who were already diagnosed, reading their experiences and quietly lining them up against my own. Then one night, buried deep in a thread, I found a comment. A woman mentioned that she had finally found care in Montana. I did a little investigative light stalking of her page—completely non-creepy, obviously—and realized that in the fourth-largest state in the country, she lived only about an hour away from me. That felt like a breakthrough. A real-life, real-time one.

I reached out to her, and that's how I found the specialist she sees, who just happened to be in the same town I live in. I remember thinking, This can't be real. It felt like an actual miracle was unfolding.

And still... I almost cancelled the appointment. When you spend an agonizing number of years being told no, being dismissed, sent away, or having very real symptoms blamed on made-up anxiety, you start to brace yourself for it. You expect the door to close again. After coming so far—after doing so much of the work on my own—I wasn't sure I was ready to sit across from another doctor and hear it all dismissed one more time. I had no other rocks to look under or doors to peek behind. This was my very last option and chance for a real diagnosis.

But this doctor didn't send me away. She didn't tell me no. My EDS specialist told me exactly what was happening to my body—exactly what I had felt, deep down, that I already knew. It almost didn't feel real. And yet, hearing it confirmed by a medical professional was a seismic shift. One sentence changed the entire landscape of my life.

Because Ehlers-Danlos Syndrome covers a wide spectrum of symptoms, co-morbidities, and degrees of severity, so much so that even with a proper diagnosis, the real work falls to the patient. You have to learn how it shows up in your body. The diagnosis is a milestone, yes, but it's not a solution. There's no cure. No magic pill. You're still treating symptoms, managing damage, adapting as it evolves.

Being formally diagnosed was a true turning point in my lifelong and chaotic ongoing medical saga. It changed everything. I left that appointment with a stack of lab orders, several new medications, a pile of new supplements to take, what could've passed for a full-time job's worth of referrals, and a mountain of real information to process. She explained that moving forward, interventions would not cure me by any means, as there is no cure, but treatments are meant to otherwise increase my quality of life a little bit at a time. And she explained just how little: we're talking five to ten percent here and there, maybe.

Knowledge really is power. You'd think that when something is wrong with your body, the obvious, natural move would be to go to the doctor. You don't need to have the answers—that's supposed to be their job. They examine, test, diagnose, and treat. Simple, right? Not for EDS patients. Not for a very long time. To be more specific, the average amount of time it takes for an EDS patient is conservatively ten to twelve years, but in my age group of mid-thirties (at the time of diagnosis) and older, it can take decades.

Back then, I was dismissed, misdiagnosed, or flat-out ignored. If a physician didn't know what to do to help me, the catch-all was always an anxiety diagnosis. It was easier for so many doctors to put me in a psychological box than to admit their limitations and range of knowledge for what might actually be wrong with me. Yet not one ever offered a pathway to help navigate said "anxiety." I was just sent packing, having never exhibited any signs or symptoms of anxiety.

In the first year following my diagnosis, I had two major life-saving surgeries in different parts of the country.

Off I flew to Charleston to meet with Dr. Patel for an in-person consultation. Despite having a radiologist's report and a CD of images, costing twelve hundred dollars, Dr. Patel in South Carolina insisted on reviewing the scans himself—thank God. That kind of direct and intentional care matters. After a few questions and careful measurements, Dr. Patel looked me in the eye and said, "You need surgery next week. And do not look up."

Excuse me, what?

Validation was the first to arrive at the party. I knew something was wrong! The blackouts, the neck brace, the "non-migraine" headaches. I knew it.

Then reality busted in: my neck's extreme flexibility meant my arteries were at risk of being crushed when I looked upward. For most, that could mean temporary blindness or a stroke. For people like me, it could mean severed nerves. Severed arteries. The risk of death.

The official spokesanimal of Ehlers-Danlos Syndrome is a zebra because these animals embody an old medical adage: "When you hear hoofbeats, think horses, not zebras." Doctors are taught to look for common diagnoses first; however, EDS patients are the rare exceptions, the unexpected "zebras" that still need recognition, with the added meaning that no two zebras have identical stripes, just like the varied symptoms in the EDS community.

The only solution for me: spinal fusion from the occiput to C3. No questions. No delay. I politely informed Dr. Patel that my insurance would take issue with a procedure that huge and out of network in one week. He gave me two weeks to get all the details worked out, and insisted I absolutely wait no longer than that.

With Validation and Reality already sipping cocktails in the corner, Fear slipped into the party like the uninvited cretin it is—creeping up behind me with a long list of spiraling thoughts. Two weeks? I have a family. Where am I supposed to stay? My husband has to be home with the kids—they've got school, he's got work, and he supports my busted ass! This is out-of-network. Insurance is going to be a nightmare. How long is recovery?

What if I accidentally look up?

Because this care was out-of-network, the hospital required a five-thousand-dollar down payment before they'd even schedule the procedure.

So, now I had two weeks to find five grand in cash, buy two plane tickets, secure a place to recover after discharge, and cover all the other costs stacked like Jenga blocks on a wobbly card table. I needed about ten thousand dollars total.

That's when Sadness arrived. Quiet. Heavy. No entrance announcement—just slipped in, sank onto the couch, and sighed. That bitch is tired.

I had to fly home and figure it out, juggling EDS, additional conditions, and the general dumpster fire of the Human Condition. Oh, I'm sorry, did I not mention that this was October 2020? With the pandemic in full force?

As soon as the plane touched down, so did I. All I wanted was to crawl into bed and pretend none of it was happening. But instead, I bounced between two places: on the phone coordinating this next bullshit chapter of my life, and in the shower crying. Sometimes both. Yeah. Real glamorous.

So there I am, two weeks after returning from my first trip to Charleston: standing on my front porch, bags packed, my oldest daughter at school, my youngest daughter at a friend's house, my husband at work, and I'm waiting for my ride to the airport. The difficult goodbyes have been said to my family, the hugs hugged, kisses kissed, and tears cried. My phone rings. It's the hospital in South Carolina. Suddenly, $5,000 might not be enough for them to let me in for a surgery that, by the way, is required to keep me alive.

I end up in a three-way call with the hospital and my insurance case manager, begging them to remember I did everything they asked and secured payment. I need to get on that damn plane. They say they'll call back with a decision.

I hang up, heart pounding, sitting on my porch alone, unsure if I'm about to fly to life-saving surgery or just...sit there. Give up. Lie down on the ground. At least from down there, I can see the clouds again without having to look up, per se.

With barely a minute to spare before I'd miss my flight, the phone rings again. It's a go. Get to the airport. Get on the plane. For.

Fuck's. Sake. Oh, and part of the hospital's pre-op protocol? A psych eval to make sure my mental health is aligned enough to promote healing. Because nothing helps mental wellness quite like being held hostage by a hospital bill and barely making it to your own life-or-death surgery.

Charleston, here we go.

The afternoon before surgery, my husband made it to South Carolina to be with me for three days. It felt like a lifetime since I'd seen him. For the first week, my only job had been to go to preliminary appointments and sit in my quiet Airbnb, trying to stay calm in the echo chamber of silence and loneliness. Every minute stretched into an hour.

Anxiety, the uninvited friend, did show up now, ironically, and tried to keep me company, but that never goes well. Obviously. I felt so intensely alone. So sad. I missed my family deeply with every part of me. But even through the weight of it, I reminded myself: I can do hard things. Hard things for my heart. Hard things for my body.

I kept repeating:
I am capable. I am stronger than I think.
I have to show everyone I can do this.
I have to show my kids I will fight to stay with them.
So many people helped me get here; I can't let them down.

That's also when I realized I kind of suck at self-pep talks. They always ended in tears. But hey, at least I had time to practice. Still do. There's no manual for moments like this. So when the pep talk ran its short course, I leaned on gratitude. It stretches further. It steadies the ground.

How lucky am I to have found a doctor who finally gave me the answer I'd been chasing for years? How grateful am I for the people who showed up, who pulled strings and rallied to make a huge fundraiser happen so I could be here, getting this surgery in time? How amazing is it to have a neurosurgeon who is both wildly skilled and genuinely kind; someone who actually cares?

The night before surgery, I ordered my husband some of the best BBQ I'd found in South Carolina and let him enjoy it while I soaked in the comfort of his presence. The next morning, we headed to the hospital. Pandemic restrictions were in full force. Every hoop had been jumped through. We were brought back to pre-op, where they started hooking me up to IVs and monitors, drawing labs, and asking the long list of protocol questions.

The nurses were kind. Human. It made all the difference. Honestly, I don't get too scared before surgery. I have had twenty-eight of them, to date, thanks to EDS, with more on the horizon. That anesthesia countdown part? It may be weird, but it's my (only) favorite part. I always want to see how far I can get before I wake up, and it's over.

I hoped those calm, kind nurses helped my husband, too. It's never easy for him. My heart has always ached more for him than for myself. It always will. There's a certain look he gets every time before I go back. It breaks my heart into a thousand sharp pieces. And I've never believed I'm the strong one here. If I had to watch him or our kids go through what I've endured, I don't know how I'd function. I don't know if I'd even get out of bed.

They are the real heroes. The ones who save the day again and again. They've never given up on me. Believe it or not, a lot of people with illnesses like mine are abandoned. Left behind by friends and family who cannot bear the weight or the burden. But not my family. I have never had to endure this alone. Even when doctors didn't believe me. But my husband did. He never thought for one minute that I was crazy.

How lucky am I?

The surgery went as planned. My memory from the hospital is fragmented at best. I don't even remember saying goodbye to my husband—my person—when he had to leave me to fly home to be with the kids. That part still breaks my heart a little. A lot.

After I was discharged, I moved into another Airbnb where a couple of amazing friends who flew all the way from Montana took over caregiving duty while I recovered enough to be cleared for the flight home. My memories from that time are like flickering snapshots: waking up in searing pain, slipping back into sleep, rinse, repeat.

In the airport, headed for home, I was in a wheelchair, drugged to the moon, just trying to exist. That's when my friend leaned over and told me the bartender had stopped her and asked, "Is she paralyzed or disabled or something?"

Apparently, that did not sit well with me.

Cue the Beyoncé moment. You know the dance break in Single Ladies where she struts forward with her palm sharply slicing through the air back and forth? Yeah. I stood straight up out of my wheelchair and did that. All the way past the bar. On pain meds. In full surgical recovery. With something to prove to a complete stranger. Let's be honest. It probably looked less "Beyoncé power move" and more "angry baby giraffe in a neck brace," But I was fueled by pure indignation and narcotics, so in my mind, I nailed it. Go Me.

I've taken two major lessons from my ongoing EDS struggles:

One: Life-altering illness, especially one with no cure, requires discipline. Your brain now carries the weight your body once managed with ease and thoughtlessness. And that takes discipline—to own it. To adapt, even when you don't want to. Even when it's easier to point a finger at something you didn't ask for and couldn't control. Like illness.

Two: You can determine what's out of your control—and let that shit go. Do yourself the favor. Stop sweating the small stuff and focus on what you can actually manage. And for that matter, sweat the big stuff as big as one should; feel all your feelings to their fullest—and then let it go, too. Illness isn't a free pass to give up, to lie in a hole and start scooping dirt over yourself like it's already over. You're far from done.

Get out of the hole. Bury the things that no longer serve you, and live your life on your own terms. Stop just existing. My greatest fear isn't dying—it's existing without ever truly living. Forgetting that when life changes, we're allowed to rewrite the rules. None of us gets out of this thing alive. In the end, we're all "terminal." The real question is whether we live while we're here. That's why I want to be what I call: "Terminally Alive."

A diagnosis changes you. You're not who you used to be. Good. Accept it. Be part of your own evolution because it's critical. You are the main character of your life. So, be alive—truly live— and find what motivates you now. Realize that what worked before may not work anymore. But just because you don't know the answer yet, it doesn't mean there isn't one.

You have nothing to prove to anybody else. Do you really need other people to notice that you did a good job? Or is it enough to know, deep down, that you did something you can feel good about?

When your body is failing you, it does not mean you have failed.

Ever.

Work with what you've got, your heart, your mind, your reason. Choose to be exceptional. And don't ignore the opportunities that disguise themselves as challenges. Sometimes, those are the ones that will save you.

ABOUT THE AUTHOR

Melissa Burns lives in Montana with her husband, two teenage daughters, and a lively collection of animals that includes a dog, cats, chickens, and goats. Her career path has been anything but linear—ranging from a classically French-trained chef to an EMT, and later the owner of her own business, *Girlwood*, where she built a devoted following creating wood-burned art from small, intricate pieces to full-scale installations for businesses.

After a mysterious, life-altering illness forced her to step away from her work, Melissa became her own fiercest advocate in the search for answers. She was ultimately diagnosed with Ehlers-Danlos Syndrome, a genetic connective tissue disorder that reshaped every aspect of her life.

She is currently writing her memoir, *Terminally Alive*, a deeply personal account of her journey to diagnosis and the reality of living with an incurable condition. Through her writing,

Melissa aims to educate, validate those navigating long and complex diagnostic journeys, and offer a perspective rooted in honesty, resilience, and hope. Her work speaks not only to those living with chronic illness but also to caregivers, loved ones, medical professionals, and anyone searching for understanding and validation.

Your Story Is Not Over Yet

by Lauren-Ashleigh Whitaker

I sat in the bathtub, knees tucked to my chest, hands cradling my head, and let the tears fall freely. The water around me had long gone cold, but I barely noticed. I wanted to scream, to let the sound match the chaos inside, but I couldn't bear the thought of scaring my husband or son in the next room. So instead, I swallowed the sound and let the silence hold my pain.

Today was a ten on the pain scale. It felt like labor contractions, except instead of birthing life, I was birthing knives. The difference between these contractions and the ones that bring a baby into the world is cruelly simple: labor ends. This doesn't. There would be no swaddled miracle at the end of this suffering. Only another day of enduring it.

Most days, my lower abdominal and back pain hovered around a five, sometimes a seven. Manageable, if you can call it that. But days like today, the pain that reached the tens, those were the ones that broke something open inside me. The ones where the pain became louder than my thoughts, where I wondered how I could possibly get through another minute, let alone another day.

And then, out of nowhere, I heard my mom's voice in my head, words she'd said to me so many times growing up: *"God gives you what you can handle."*

Sometimes those words felt like a battle cry, like a sword I could carry into the storm. Other times, usually through teenage tears sprawled on the floor, I'd mutter, *"Well, you can tell God I've had enough."*

Today was one of those days.

Only this time, it wasn't a dramatic teenage eye roll. It was a prayer from the bottom of the pit. A begging, pleading kind of moment. A conversation with God that came out more like a cry. Helplessness filled my bones and anger in my soul: *"Where are you? Why haven't you taken this pain away?"*

This was my third surgery to remove endometriosis adhesions. Three times they'd gone in, searching for the cause of this invisible war inside me. And yet, here I was again, bleeding, aching, questioning everything I thought I believed about faith, strength, and what it means to endure.

But getting here wasn't sudden; it was years in the making.

I'd already become a trial-and-error case, like so many women with endometriosis do. I'd collected victories along the way, bursts of reprieve after each surgery. Moments I thought I'd won, that gave me back a little bit of hope, but each win felt like a temporary ceasefire in a war that refused to end.

Four years earlier, I had just had my son. I was a new mom, running on love, coffee, and the kind of exhaustion that hums in your bones. Many of my symptoms could have been brushed off as postpartum chaos, brain fog, body aches, headaches, fatigue, but deep down, I knew these weren't new. They'd been whispering long before pregnancy; now, they were screaming.

I was constantly bloated, in pain after eating anything, bone-tired, foggy-headed, and barely hanging on. My primary doctor ran a basic blood panel that revealed vitamin deficiencies and a high ANA level, a red flag for autoimmune issues like lupus or rheumatoid arthritis. I was sent to a rheumatologist, who barely looked up from the chart before confidently diagnosing me with lupus.

When I tried to explain my doubts, they brushed them off. "Trust us, it fits; we're the doctors." They prescribed medication, a vegan diet, and a future I didn't recognize. Six months later, I was worse. My body was shutting down, my muscles weakening, and my hope unraveling.

At my second appointment, my husband joined me. The doctor turned to him and said, "You should start looking at one-story houses before stairs become an issue."

That moment was surreal. I wanted to scream at this doctor, *"You're talking about my life while I'm sitting right here!"* Instead, I waited until I got to the car to let out the fury that had been brewing inside of me- the tears flowed, gasping for air in between, moments of anger and heartbreak. After this breakdown, I made a decision: I wasn't accepting this storyline. I wasn't ready to be written out of my own story. This was not my ending.

With my husband's support, I found a new doctor who took a comprehensive, holistic approach. The new tests showed the same high ANA levels, but none of the markers for lupus. She took me off the medication the rheumatologist had given me, and encouraged me to eat meat again. Within weeks, I started regaining energy, muscle tone, and a glimmer of the version of me that I wanted to be.

But the pain—the deep, unrelenting, doubled over, twisting the knife into my uterus and lower back pain didn't leave. It intensified.

Around that time, my sister had undergone surgery for endometriosis. She recognized the look in my eyes, the combination of exhaustion and defiance. She told me, "You need to see my surgeon."

That conversation led to my first laparoscopy. The surgeon agreed that my symptoms aligned with endometriosis, and we scheduled the procedure. Each surgery gave me a little bit of relief, a few months of breathing room, and when you live with chronic pain, even a few months can feel like winning the lottery.

So yes, I said yes to a second. And then a third.

Throughout all of this, I was also trying to preserve the dream of another child. My uterus and ovaries symbolized hope, and I wasn't ready to let that go. But with each procedure, the hope dimmed.

By the third surgery, I had unknowingly become an experiment. My surgeon decided to "tack" my uterus to my abdominal wall, believing its tilted position might be the cause of my pain. Instead, he created a new hell. I woke up feeling like my insides were on fire, my uterus literally tethered to the side of my body.

I felt grateful and betrayed in the same breath. Thankful someone tried to help, furious that your body became a lesson plan.

And yet, even that wasn't the darkest moment…The pain was unbearable. Life-halting. Identity-cracking. Living like this day to day felt impossible.

What's strange about living with an *invisible illness* is that it doesn't announce itself. There are no casts or bruises, no visible proof for others to point to and say, "Oh, that's why she's struggling." The battle happens quietly, beneath the surface. It's a cruel paradox: your body is at war, yet to the outside world you look completely fine.

Each morning became a choice: do I let the world see the wreckage, or do I pull myself together and step into the day like a soldier heading into battle? Most days, I chose the latter. Not because I was fine, but because it was the only dignity I had left of my old self. Getting dressed, putting on makeup, showing up—it wasn't vanity; it was defiance. My armor. My way of saying, *I may not control what's happening inside my body, but I can still choose how I show up in it.*

People often told me how strong I was. And yes, maybe I was, but the truth is, "strong" was the costume I wore to survive. It was how I kept showing up for my son, who still needed his mom to show him love; for my husband, who deserved more than my pain; for my family and friends, who kept believing in my comeback; for my clients, who looked to me for hope. But most of all, now I know I was showing up for *me*. The version of myself I refused to lose, the woman I was trying to become and find, no matter how loud the pain got.

Still, beneath that strength, I was unraveling. I knew I couldn't live this way forever. Every day felt like walking through quicksand, each movement a battle, each smile a negotiation. I needed a lifeline.

That's when I found Dr. Levine.

Through research and a few divine nudges, there was Dr. Levine, a highly regarded endometriosis specialist whose California calm was a balm to my nervous system. He was everything my previous surgeon wasn't: attentive, kind, the kind of doctor who spoke *to* me, not *around* me.

After thorough testing and imaging, he confirmed what others had missed: in addition to endometriosis, I likely had *adenomyosis*, when endometrial tissue burrows into the uterine wall itself, turning the organ into its own source of suffering. Most likely, this was why I was in such pain previously. But then the source of knife-wrenching torture was compounded when my uterus had also been unnaturally tacked to the side of my body, in my last surgery, leading to no relief in sight.

His recommendation was clear: a hysterectomy. Removal of my uterus. The only real hope for relief.

But the word "removal" echoed like a loss I couldn't name. Removing my uterus meant removing the possibility of another child. It meant taking away something I'd long associated with womanhood, creation, and identity.

And that's how we arrive back at the bathtub.

The pain was unbearable, but the fear was louder than my heartbeat.

I was terrified the surgery wouldn't work. After all, my record was zero for three. What reason did I have to believe the fourth would be any different? And this time, the cost felt heavier. I wasn't just risking another failed attempt at relief; I was losing a part of myself. The future I once imagined. The life I had been quietly, relentlessly working toward for as long as I could remember.

A future I had been told to want.

Grow up. Get married. Buy a house. Have two children, just like your parents did. Follow the outline. Complete the checklist. This is what fulfillment looks like. This is how you fit into the world.

As I sat there in cold water, I realized how deeply I had absorbed that story, how much I believed that if I just endured long enough, if I completed the steps correctly, happiness would eventually arrive. But now my body was asking me to let go of that version of the future entirely.

This wasn't just another surgery to survive. It was a reckoning with the unknown. A grief for what I might lose. A fear of becoming a shell of the woman I once was, or worse, losing her altogether.

So I cried. And I prayed. Maybe I begged. I definitely cursed.

(If there's a soundtrack to this moment, it would be "Desperate" by Jamie MacDonald and Lauren Daigle—that ache-filled space where faith isn't polished or pretty, just raw and pleading.)

I told God I needed a break. That I couldn't take much more. That I was tired of being the strong one. I asked if He still saw me in all of this because I was losing sight of myself. Losing clarity on who I was, who I could become, and how I was supposed to keep going.

I wouldn't say I wanted to die.
But I was struggling to live.

Pain had taught me how to survive.
It hadn't taught me how to feel.

Waking up from the fourth surgery felt different.

There was discomfort, yes, but it was a pain I could manage. And beneath it, something I hadn't felt in years: relief. Not certainty. Not celebration. Just the quiet sense that this suffering may not be the monster under the bed, the rest of my life. A flicker of hope that this pain might not be endless after all. For the first time, I believed recovery was possible.

Months later, my husband looked at me for a long moment before speaking. When I asked what he was thinking, he said, "There you are. You're back. I can finally see life in your eyes again."

The words landed deeper than I expected, and tears began to flow before I could stop them. His comment was heart-opening in all the right ways—because he was right. For the first time in years, I could see myself too. The armor that had protected me for years fell, unleashing years of heartbreak, anguish, frustration, and sadness, all while experiencing relief and pure happiness.

For five years, my life had been shaped by survival. Five years of doubting my body, my instincts, my sanity, being dismissed, minimized, and told my pain was something to tolerate rather than understand. I had been advised by my OB-GYN to drink wine to make intimacy easier. I had been told by doctors that it was all in my head. And slowly, quietly, I began to question myself.

There are moments from my son's early years I don't hold as clearly as I wish I did. I know I was there, but I wasn't fully present. Pain has a way of stealing attention, of blurring memory, of shrinking life down to endurance.

That grief still finds me.

But so does gratitude.

Grateful that I'm here. Grateful that I fought to be heard. Grateful that my life is no longer consumed by surviving it. Grateful that

I get to wake up now and participate, fully, in the moments that matter. As Scripture says, *"Suffering produces perseverance; perseverance, character; and character, hope" (Romans 5:3-4).* I didn't understand that during my deepest suffering. I do now.

My struggles didn't disappear. I still manage daily health challenges. I follow protocols, adjust my diet, and listen carefully to my body. And I would endure all of it again and again, for the life I have now.

Because it was in these chapters of my story that I learned something I couldn't have learned any other way: transformation doesn't come wrapped in clarity. It comes through surrender, perseverance, and hope.

If life had gone according to my plan, I would have had more children. I wouldn't have had to grieve parts of my body, or the version of womanhood and the checklist I once believed defined my worth. But God's plan didn't follow mine. And in the choices I never would have made for myself, I discovered something truer than certainty: my strength, my grit, my grace, and the gifts I was given to support others.

I've learned that while we may create one play in the playbook, God holds the entire story.

My scars tell the truth of that story. They are not evidence of failure; they are proof of refinement. Proof that healing isn't about erasing what hurt you. It's about becoming who you were always meant to be because of it.

For a long time, I believed there was a checklist for a meaningful life. But pain has a way of interrupting performance. It exposes the difference between fitting in and belonging.

Fitting in asks you to change, to soften your truth, to mold yourself into what's expected. Belonging asks for honesty. It requires courage. Sometimes it requires standing alone. But it allows you to show up as you are and be received.

I was never meant to fit into a life that required me to abandon myself. I was meant to belong to my body, my faith, my becoming.

We all carry scars. Some are visible. Others live quietly beneath the surface. At first, they feel like they own us. Over time, we learn to live with them. Then, if we're willing, we learn to let them connect us to ourselves and to one another.

Because suffering in a broken world is hard enough. Suffering alone is harder.

If you are in the middle of something that feels unbearable—if you are exhausted, disoriented, or losing hope, please hear this: the struggle does not mean you've been forgotten. It means something is still being molded.

If you are still here, still fighting, still searching for hope, then the story is not finished. God isn't done with you yet.

Your story is still unfolding.

ABOUT THE AUTHOR

Lauren-Ashleigh "L.A." Whitaker is a nationally recognized therapist, mindset coach, and speaker with nearly 15 years of experience in supporting people move from fear-based striving to wholehearted living. She is the founder of Sea-Change Health & Wellness, where she works with individuals, couples, athletes, entrepreneurs, and high-performing leaders who are tired of achieving everything on the outside while quietly seeking more on the inside. Her approach blends clinical therapy, CBT, EMDR, mindset coaching, and somatic practices; all in service of the same mission: helping people identify their core values, embrace their superpowers, and create lives that feel as genuine as they look impressive.

But her greatest education has come from living it herself. A wife and mother, L.A. knows firsthand the balancing act of showing up fully in multiple arenas—and she brings that real-world understanding to every conversation. Off the clock, you'll find her lifting weights, getting in a Pilates class, dragging her friends to the latest health trend, hosting a low-key game night, planning a date night out, or cheering her heart out as a proud sports mom in the bleachers. She knows what it means to show up for everyone around you and forget to show up for yourself—to wear "strong" like a costume and what it feels like to finally take it off.

She meets every client exactly where they are, with compassion, honesty, and the deep belief that wholeness is not something you earn—it is something you return to. As she puts it: *"My clients don't just want another achievement. They want a life they're excited to wake up to, and finally feel like it's their own."*

I Was Never Meant to Shrink

by Erin Darling

I was the fat kid.

My body was my entire identity before I had the chance to form one of my own. I learned early that it determined how I was treated, how accepted I felt, and how much space I believed I was allowed to take up. I was an easy target and an emotional sponge; a perfect combo to satisfy and reinforce the relentless bullying in my life. I was only eight years old when my entire self-concept was formed, and it wasn't good.

I was also highly sensitive and living with undiagnosed ADHD, which meant my internal world was loud, emotional, and overwhelming. By the time I hit my teen years, the shame of simply being "too much" lived on a constant loop in my mind, and the only way I knew to escape it was through binge eating. Binge eating actually began many years prior, as my one and only coping tool.

But it was during my final year of middle school that things took an even darker turn. Up until that very specific day, the teasing I endured had been quiet and insidious, happening in whispers at the back of the classroom, just out of the teacher's earshot. That day, however, it moved front and center, turning me into a circus-like spectacle for my entire PE class.

In my mind's eye, I can still see the field: classmates spread far and wide, the brightness of the grass, and my teacher assigning me as the goalie. Me. I was probably the most unsporty girl in the group, yet I was handed the intimidating responsibility of making sure our team didn't lose. Beyond the pressure of the role, I was terrified of catching the ball, but also missing the ball would be even worse. This was because the net was positioned at the top of a very long, very steep hill. The kind of hill that feels epic for sledding, but dangerous for everything else

As soon as the game started, it was obvious I wasn't going to block a single shot. Each time a player kicked the ball, full force, it sailed right past me and went rolling down what felt like the longest, steepest hill in the world. As goalie, it was my job to chase after it and retrieve it, giving the other twenty-plus girls in my class a front-row seat.

At age thirteen, I played zero sports. I had even quit trick-or-treating years earlier because I simply couldn't keep up with my friends. Because remember, I was the fat kid. This moment was doomed from the start. Still, I ran as hard as I could, determined to please my team. When I brought the ball back, I had a small moment of pride knowing that I had done something so physically demanding.

That moment of relief was short-lived because what I didn't know was that while I was running, the girls left on the field were conspiring. They decided to form an alliance of sorts to make me run that hill as many times as they could. And they did. And so *I* did.

Shot after shot missed. Up and down the hill I went, until my asthma kicked in and my emotions came flooding out.

Somewhere in the middle of it all, I heard a classmate say, "Good. She needs to run!" And even though years earlier I had been called a pig, disgusting, and lazy, that comment has left the deepest scar.

Eventually, my teacher noticed what was happening and put an end to it. But by then, the damage had already been done. That day wasn't the end of the teasing; it was the beginning of something far more harmful.

That same night, my bulimia began. I decided, with a fierce kind of certainty, that no one, and I mean *no one,* would ever make me feel that insignificant or vulnerable again.

Bulimia became my ultimate escape. I would fill myself to unbearable levels within minutes, fueled by the intoxicating promise of purging immediately afterward. Purging came in many forms, and I explored them all. My days became a relentless cycle of vomiting, laxatives, diuretics, and overexercising, swinging wildly between deprivation and relief, control and collapse.

And I wasn't only purging. I was restricting. Tightening my self-inflicted rules as armor to protect myself. If I could perfect my body, maybe I could avoid being wounded again. The weight came off quickly, just before high school started. I was young, and my body responded fast. And almost overnight, the way people treated me changed. Compliments and attention flooded me, reinforcing the belief that smaller was, in fact, better.

That approval was powerful. It made the illness feel effective. Even successful.

As if that weren't enough, I also began drinking and partying at fourteen. I loved the release alcohol gave me, how easily it softened the edges of my world and numbed the sadness I didn't know how to carry.

Yet on the outside, I looked like a typical American teen, high-achieving and outgoing, but inside, I was trapped in a dangerous loop of self-loathing that reached its pinnacle in college, where I hid all of my harmful behaviors effortlessly. For the first time, there was no parental supervision—no one noticing if I skipped meals or questioning my over-exercising. Without anyone looking closely, my destructive habits blended seamlessly into the chaos of student life.

Over the years in undergrad, I became incredibly skilled at appearing "put together" while privately living by rigid, exhausting, and restrictive rules. Before heading out to social gatherings with friends, I would pre-calculate the day, allowing myself a measly 400 calories total in food, so I could "afford" alcoholic drinks later.

When out, I often avoided food altogether. I felt an intense sense of control. It was almost intoxicating, stronger than anything in my glass. But my body always knew. I remember the dull ache in my stomach, a hollow discomfort I tried to ignore. Sometimes it was nausea. Sometimes it was sharp cramps. Sometimes it was just an unsettled feeling, almost as if my body and brain were confused. But I told myself it was normal, strong, controlled, and what I had to do to fit in.

So, that's what I did all through college. Even as the president of my art education association. Even while in leadership, organizing events in my sorority and achieving good grades. On paper, I was thriving, but on the inside, I was running on very little nourishment and a constant undercurrent of self-criticism.

When I was twenty-five, I reached a pivotal breaking point. I was finally beginning to recognize just how disordered my thoughts and behaviors had become. I was exhausted from living in the food prison I had locked myself into years before. All that time, I thought I was fighting back, but the truth was, every time I punished and shrank myself, the bullies were still winning. They no longer had to say the words. I had learned to say them to myself.

I was worn down by the endless cycle of restriction during the week, unraveling on the weekends, and relentlessly chasing the next new diet. The rush of discovering a "better" way to eat felt intoxicating and even hopeful, but ultimately addictive. And deep down, I knew something had to change.

The realization came slowly, in the quiet moments alone with my thoughts. I began to look outside of myself and understand that if I didn't change my mindset, I would inevitably pass these patterns on to my children, perpetuating the cycle of self-loathing and shame that so many women carry from one generation to the next. The thought of contributing to that legacy, rather than breaking it, became too big a burden to bear.

I also carried a deep inner knowing that one day I would be given the gift of raising girls. And I knew I could not pass down the belief that women must shrink to be loved.

At this point, restricting and purging were familiar. Automatic. Almost easy. Healing, on the other hand, felt unbearable. It meant feeling *everything*. Letting go of control. Facing the parts of myself I had worked so hard to hide. But I owed it to my unborn daughters to do the hard work. And even more importantly, I owed it to myself.

And as if someone flipped a switch, my approach shifted. I threw away the diet books, calorie trackers, and journals that had defined my worth by numbers on a page. I can still remember the enormous relief I felt as I filled a trash bag—almost as if I was finally able to take off a heavy backpack I had been carrying for most of my life.

I then worked internally to stop the self-deprecating remarks that had long disguised themselves as humor. I could no longer justify verbally tearing down the one person who had always been there: me.

I began to sit with my inner world, confronting shame and fear instead of masking it with food or alcohol. Therapy, meditation, journaling, yoga, and any healing practice I could find became tools, not rules, in the process of reclaiming myself.

It wasn't instant or easy. Change never is. I wish I could say I never had relapses or that the two beautiful daughters I did, in fact, give birth to, never faced struggle. I wish I could say they live in a world where their bodies aren't measured, compared, and critiqued. A world where being a girl doesn't come with quiet rules about shrinking, pleasing, accommodating, and staying small.

But the truth is, being a girl is—and has always been—hard. We have been fighting to be seen and heard for who we are, not what we look like, since the beginning of time. And as much as I want to eradicate that deficit we are placed in, I can't. But I can work hard to be someone they are proud of. Someone who admits when she's wrong. Someone who takes ownership. Someone who no longer glorifies restriction or silence. Someone who teaches her daughters that their needs are not inconveniences. That they do not have to people-please to be loved.

My dysfunctional inner world, narrowed by body image, self-improvement, and constant judgment of myself and everyone around me, was small and flat. It held no color or texture, only a shallow well of quiet unhappiness. I wanted to become someone who learned to be more interesting than the shallowness society demanded from me.

Being the woman I am still evolving into today has taken fearless dedication. I am proud that I am not a perfect person or mother, but a present one. A woman who continues to grow and change so they can learn they are allowed to do the same.

I no longer play small to make other people comfortable. I am not afraid to speak up, to disagree, to use my voice, and to take up space in a room.

The energy that once went toward shrinking my body now goes toward expanding my life. Toward meaningful work. Toward honest relationships. Toward raising girls who see a woman who trusts herself and lives as her most true, authentic self.

There is depth here now. There is color. There is conviction.

And if I could go back, I would find that younger version of me. Little Erin.

I would sit beside her, the girl who believed she was too much and not enough at the same time. The girl who thought her body was the problem.

I would wrap her up in my arms, and I would tell her she was never a problem to be fixed. That she was bright and bubbly. She was deserving and worthy. She was funny and feisty. She was sensitive and strong.

She was never meant to shrink to fit the world. She was meant to grow beyond it. And so are you.

ABOUT THE AUTHOR

Erin Darling is a behavior change coach, former educator, and the founder of Mindset Nutrition, where she helps high-achieving, people-pleasing professionals break free from the exhausting cycle of perfectionism, food control, and self-criticism. She holds dual master's degrees in education and nutrition, and is a certified corporate wellness coach as well as an eating disorder intuitive therapy coach.

For years, Erin mastered the art of appearing "put together." Beneath the surface, she lived by rigid, punishing food rules; carefully calculating, restricting, and striving to feel in control. What looked like discipline from the outside was, in reality, a quiet battle with disordered patterns and an inner voice that never seemed satisfied. Eventually, the control she clung to became the very thing that kept her stuck.

Her breaking point became her turning point.

Today, Erin uses both her professional expertise and lived experience to help others step out of the same patterns. Her work blends behavior change, compassion, and deep mindset shifts to help clients rebuild trust with their bodies, prioritize themselves without guilt, and create a life that feels as good on the inside as it looks on the outside.

Afterword

by Sisi Surgant

When you reach the end of a mosaic, there is no single piece that completes it, no final moment where everything suddenly makes sense. What settles in instead is a quiet realization that it has been forming all along, through every story, every choice, every step that brought it together.

What you have just read is not a collection of endings. These stories do not close in perfect lines, because healing does not move that way. It deepens over time, often in the quiet, unseen moments where real change begins. And still, something powerful has taken shape here.

You have witnessed women who chose to stand in their stories, who allowed everything they have lived through to become part of their strength. Each voice stands fully on its own, and together they create something that carries weight, presence, and meaning.

A beautiful mosaic.

Every piece holds its own history, its own beauty, its own place. When they come together, they create something richer, something you can feel the moment you see it. And if you felt something while reading these pages, that was not by accident.

Maybe you recognized a part of yourself. A memory, a truth, a feeling you have carried quietly. Something that has been waiting for you to see it differently. Because you are not starting from nothing.

You are remembering. Remembering your strength, your voice, your depth. The part of you that has always been there, even in the moments you doubted it. You are allowed to grow, to evolve, and to become more. And at the same time, there is a power within you that has never left you.

This mosaic does not end here. It continues in every woman who chooses to own her story, to carry it with intention, and to shape it into something meaningful. There is no final piece. There is only the moment you realize this, you were always meant for more.